The media's watching Vau... Here's a sampling of our coverage.

"Unflinching, fly-on-the-wall reports... No one gets past company propaganda to the nitty-gritty inside dope better than these guys."
— *Knight-Ridder newspapers*

"Best way to scope out potential employers...Vault has sharp insight into corporate culture and hiring practices."
— *Yahoo! Internet Life*

"Vault has become a de facto Internet outsourcer of the corporate grapevine."
— *Fortune*

"For those hoping to climb the ladder of success, [Vault's] insights are priceless."
— *Money.com*

"Another killer app for the Internet."
— *New York Times*

"If only the company profiles on the top sites would list the 'real' information... Sites such as Vault do this, featuring insights and commentary from employees and industry analysts."
— *The Washington Post*

"A rich repository of information about the world of work."
— *Houston Chronicle*

VAULT
> the most trusted name in career information™

D0639785

CAREER
GUIDE

VAULT CASE INTERVIEW

PRACTICE GUIDE 2

MORE CASE INTERVIEWS

© 2008 Vault.com Inc.

CAREER
GUIDE

VAULT CASE INTERVIEW

PRACTICE GUIDE 2

MORE CASE INTERVIEWS

CASE
INTERVIEW

RISHI MARWAH, SRIDHAR PARAMESHWARAN,
ROBERT VUJOVICH AND THE STAFF OF VAULT

© 2008 Vault.com Inc.

Copyright © 2008 by Vault.com Inc. All rights reserved.

All information in this book is subject to change without notice. Vault makes no claims as to the accuracy and reliability of the information contained within and disclaims all warranties. No part of this book may be reproduced or transmitted in any form or by any means, electronic or mechanical, for any purpose, without the express written permission of Vault.com Inc.

Vault, the Vault logo, and "The Most Trusted Name in Career Information™" are trademarks of Vault.com Inc.

For information about permission to reproduce selections from this book, contact Vault.com Inc., 150 West 22nd Street, New York, NY 10011, (212) 366-4212.

Library of Congress CIP Data is available.

ISBN 13 : 978-1-58131-546-2

ISBN 10 : 1-58131-546-5

Printed in the United States of America

ACKNOWLEDGMENTS

We are extremely grateful to Vault's entire staff for all their help in the editorial, production and marketing processes. Vault also would like to acknowledge the support of our investors, clients, employees, family and friends. Thank you!

Table of Contents

INTRODUCTION   1

Basic Structure of a Case Interview 1

Do's and Don'ts in the Case 4

Basic Structure of the Non-Case Part of the Interview 7

Do's and Don'ts of the Non-Case Part of the Interview 9

Practicing Interviewing 10

Case Interview Categories 12

SAMPLE CASES   17

Amusement Park Case 19

Bicycle Manufacturer Case 25

B2B Fertilizer Manufacturer Acquisition Case 31

Chinese Chemical Market Case 37

Coffee Chain Market Entry Case 42

Consumer Products Growth Strategy Case 46

Credit Card Company Revenue Growth Case 51

EU Customs Brokers Case 56

Eyewear Chain Case 61

Health Care CPG Consumer Loyalty Program Case 65

Housing Loans Market Entry Case 71

IT Benchmarking and Business Alignment Case 77

IT Outsourcing Strategy Case 83

Medical Devices Case 87

NGO Partnership Case 92

Nonprofit Brand Case 97

Norwegian Widgets Case 103

Online Gambling Case 109

Organic Fast-Food Chain Case 115

Outsourcing Commercial Debt Collection Case 122

PetCo Revenue Case 127

Pro Bono Case 131

Publishing Company M&A Case 135

Regional Bank Commercial Case 143

Satellite Communications Systems Case 149

Specialty Kitchenware Brand Case 154

Telecom Equipment/Services Provider Case 159

FINAL ANALYSIS   169

APPENDIX   173

Sample Guesstimates/Brainteasers   175

Sample Non-Case Interview Questions   176

Acing the Case: Checklist   181

Introduction

For better or for worse, the case interview is, in many ways, the biggest hurdle to a job at a consulting firm. If you ever want to be a consultant—or a strategic planner, a corporate or business development manager, or many other strategic roles in business—a case interview may be a screening tactic that you'll have to excel at in order to get the job.

Luckily, case interviewing is a learned skill. People are not born great case interviewers. Instead, successful case interviewers are those that combine the thoughtful analysis of a problem and structured thinking that they've learned over the years in other work or academic environments, with a healthy dose of case interviewing practice, to master the case interview. This book will help you with that practice. It will walk you through how to prepare for the interview: the structure of the interview, what to expect from the interview and what they're testing for in different parts of the interview, and then, it will help you practice for the case interview and help you to become successful at it!

Basic Structure of a Case Interview

The case interview is usually composed of two parts: 1) a 30- to 45-minute business case, and 2) a 30- to 45-minute "get to know you" interview. Sometimes, this format will vary slightly—with two interviewers each doing a 30-minute case and a 15-minute "get to know you" conversation. Either way, you will usually meet with two separate interviewers and do about an hour of case interviewing and a half-hour of "get to know you." (Having two interviewers allows a firm to have more than one person weigh-in their opinion on a candidate.) Most of this book is focused on how to prepare you for these, the most typical, formats for case interviews. However, it should be noted that some firms—or sometimes just some renegade interviewers—deviate from this format, and this book will address less typical case interview formats as well. But for now, onto what you're most likely to get in a case interview and how best to prepare for it.

30- to 45-minute case

The case is what you'll spend most of your time preparing for—and for good reason: you have to "pass" the case part of the interview to still be in the running. It generally consists of the following parts:

Visit the Vault Consulting Career Channel at **www.vault.com/consulting** — with insider firm profiles, message boards, the Vault Consulting Job Board and more.

VAULT CAREER LIBRARY

1

1) An introduction to a client's business problem or general question, which the interviewee is asked to structure an approach to.

2) Two to three pieces of analysis that will help lead to a result to the case. At least one of these endeavors will have a quantitative aspect, and usually one of them will require a bit of brainstorming, or option generation.

3) A conclusion in which an interviewee will be asked to summarize the case in three to five sentences, including a recommendation to the client as to what they should do.

Each of these parts to the case might include a twist, a different bit of analysis, but this basic structure forms the backbone of the 30- to 45-minute case, and once you know that this is what you can generally expect, it's easy to practice the small twists and turns that each of these parts can take.

Other interview formats

Having said all that about a typical interview format, it is also important to recognize that some firms do these things a little differently. Some have adapted the case interview to different formats, or have added their own elements into the mix to gauge candidates' abilities in other aspects of firm culture. For example, some firms use group exercises to assess a candidate's ability to work as a part of a team; other firms add an interview where a candidate is given feedback on his or her performance over the course of the process to see how he or she reacts to constructive criticism. Regardless of what the format is, these firms are still likely testing the same things as in a standard format; so, as long as you're showing the same wonderful analytical and interpersonal skills that you'll develop for more typical formats, you'll excel at these more atypical formats and tests. (Two group-format cases are included in this book for you to practice as well.)

What they're testing

The most important thing to know as you prepare for case interviews is what they're testing for in these exercises. Interviewers are not testing to see if you're the smartest person in your class—they could get a pretty good indication of that from your grades, or an IQ test. They are not testing to see if you can get "the right answer" to the case—oftentimes, there is no "right answer," or there may be more than one "right answer." (Have you ever heard the expression "There are more ways than one to skin a cat"?) Instead, they are testing for the basic skills that make a good consultant: structured thinking, creative

© 2008 Vault.com Inc.

thinking, comfort with quantitative data, and ability to synthesize data and analysis. Once you realize that those are the basic skills you have to master to be successful at any case, it's easy to practice those skills and make yourself more adept at any case interview.

Structured thinking. A lot of what consultants involves providing structured, careful thought and analysis to business executives facing complex business problems. Because of that, a substantial part of the case interview is about demonstrating clear, structured thinking.

As part of practicing cases, you'll learn to be comfortable with frameworks that apply to specific business problems (profitability = revenue - costs, the four Ps, the three Cs, etc.), but there are also more generic frameworks and tools (MECE, abc/123, etc.) in order to make all parts of the interview structured and clear.

Creative thinking/brainstorming/"thinking outside the box." Because consultants have to generate ideas on where to find sources of data, hypotheses as to what's driving a business problem and creative ways to engage clients in a consultant's process, it is important to demonstrate creative thinking—or at least significant ability in terms of idea generation—during a case interview. You will likely have at least a couple of points in the case interview where you will be asked: "What do you think is going on here?" or "Can you think of another way to look at it?" What your interviewer wants is for you to generate multiple options and then use your business logic—or some analysis during the case interview—to narrow that list of options down to a few that could be the final result of the case.

Comfort with quant. Consultants are in the business of business, and the language of business is quantitative. Consultants spend a good bit of their time working in Excel, analyzing figures, completing regression analysis, calculating percentages and ROIs, and getting from gross to net margins. Because of this, consultants have to be comfortable with numbers and quantitative analysis. While case interviewees won't be required to do complicated quantitative analysis in a case interview, they will be asked to calculate a percentage or two, do a little multiplication and division, and show that they're comfortable with numbers. This is to see that if they're asked to do a simple, "back of the envelope" calculation in front of a client, they'd be comfortable doing so.

Ability to synthesize and be decisive. In the end, after a lot of analysis and meetings—and airports—consultants are expected to actually help their clients with a business problem, and specifically, counsel them on what to do. Because of this, you should expect to make a recommendation at the end of the case. Your recommendation should not be considered a one-word "solution"

Visit the Vault Consulting Career Channel at www.vault.com/consulting — with insider firm profiles, message boards, the Vault Consulting Job Board and more.

VAULT CAREER LIBRARY

3

to the case. Instead, it should be your best-effort recommendation based on the analysis and work that you've done throughout the case interview. It should be a "data-driven" answer of a couple of sentences, which summarizes the major case points, makes a recommendation, and points to the fact that more work could be done to mitigate the risk for the client. (That's a subtle way of mentioning further sales for the firm!)

Do's and Don'ts in the Case

Besides the specific—and maybe academic—skills that they're testing for in the case interview (structured thinking, quantitative abilities, etc.), there are more subjective abilities that your interviewer is looking for. While many of the skills that they're looking for show whether or not you've prepared for your case interview and have the skills to be a good consultant, there are subjective qualities like enthusiasm, curiosity, proactivity in the conversation that help an interviewer determine whether you'd be a great consultant—and whether they'd want you on their case team. The following are some "Do's and Don'ts" to keep in mind about these more "soft skills" or abilities that you should demonstrate in the case interview.

Do's

Do drive the case.

Lean forward in your seat. Ask questions of your interviewer. Propose hypotheses as to what's going on. Too often, case interviewees expect to be fed information about the case. In reality, consultants are expected to drive analysis and learnings for their clients. Be sure to drive the case during the case interview—don't expect your interviewer to do so.

Do be enthusiastic.

You should be enjoying your case interview—it shouldn't feel like torture. Whether or not the case interview is a perfect replication of casework, who knows? But your interviewer thinks it is, and if you don't seem excited to be there, tearing through the case, your interviewer may think that you won't be excited to be a consultant.

    © 2008 Vault.com Inc.

Do ask questions.

A lot of case work is asking the right questions—not knowing all the answers immediately. Your interviewer may be holding back information that's helpful to the case, waiting for you to ask the right question, just as one has to in a case setting. Also, asking questions show curiosity and an ability to work collaboratively, two traits that a consultant needs to be effective in their work and effective working on a team.

Do show a little personality and have some fun.

A lot of what your interviewer is always testing is the airport test: "Would I want to be stuck with this person in an airport in Iowa?" Consultants spend a lot of time together, especially when traveling, and they want to hire people with whom they'll have fun, even when weather delays force them to be stuck in an airport.

Do take notes.

You'll be given a lot of data over the course of the case interview, so take notes. First, your interviewer is certainly not expecting (nor requesting) that you do everything in your head—so, don't put that expectation on yourself. Second, at the end of the case, you'll be asked to summarize your thoughts and learnings quickly, and you'll have an easier time doing that if you've been taking notes along the way. Third, if you design your notes in a way that looks like slides (with your paper in landscape position), your interviewer will see that you can "think in PowerPoint," which is what every consultant needs to do.

Do listen to your interviewer's answers to questions/hints to the case.

Your interviewers want you to succeed. They want you to do well. The entire case interview process is almost as uncomfortable for the interviewers as it is for you if you don't do well. So, they're likely to help you, give you hints to the case solution and steer you away from the wrong path if you start to go down it. Sometimes, they'll be explicit and tell you; sometimes, you can see it in the expressions on their faces and in their body language. Regardless, pay attention to your interviewer and correct your course accordingly if he or she gives you any hints that you should.

Do think out loud.

Because the case interview is not about getting the right answer, but about demonstrating clear, structured and creative thinking, it's important to think out loud. Your interviewers need to hear or see your thinking to evaluate it. So, slow down. Draw and write your thoughts on paper in clear view for your in-

Visit the Vault Consulting Career Channel at **www.vault.com/consulting** — with insider firm profiles, message boards, the Vault Consulting Job Board and more.

VAULT CAREER LIBRARY

5

terviewer to see. Think out loud. (Furthermore, if you do make a mistake in logic, assumptions or math, the only way your interviewers can know what a little mistake you made and help to correct it is if you are sharing your thought process out loud.)

Do maintain eye contact.

While you are here to tackle a case and work through a business problem, don't get so into the case that you forget all of your wonderful interpersonal skills. Remember: this is still a conversation with your interviewers, and they are still evaluating you on all the same interpersonal skills that you're evaluated on in any interview. Furthermore, by maintaining eye contact with your interviewers, you'll be able to read them for cues about how you're doing in the case!

Don'ts

Don't make assumptions.

Well, let's rephrase: don't make assumptions without making them explicit—and checking with your interviewers to see if it's a fair assumption for the case. You will likely have to have at least some data as you work through the case. But before making assumptions, ask your interviewers if they have any more data for you. If they say no, then make a reasonable assumption for the data you need to move on, ask for your interviewers' blessing and continue with the case.

Don't be afraid to correct yourself or change your mind.

Consultants have to change course in their casework all the time—usually after they've done some analysis where they prove their own hypothesis wrong—and the ego-less consultant then has to create another hypothesis and do some more analysis until he gets it right. Consultants are expected to have ideas, but not be in love with their ideas—instead, they have to let the data and analysis drive their work. You may go down the wrong path during the case interview (it may even be a part of the case to lead you to do some analysis that proves a common hypothesis wrong!), but what you should do is show them that you're flexible and responsive (and a bit humble) by changing course and continuing effectively through the case.

Don't rush!

No one ever got a consulting job by finishing a case faster than everyone else. You're not being evaluated on speed of analysis; you're being evaluated on depth of thinking and solid analysis. Yes, you'll probably be nervous during

© 2008 Vault.com Inc.

your interview, which will make you want to rush; so, practice slowing down. Take your time. Get comfortable with 30 seconds of silence as you sketch out your framework for the case, jot down your notes or write down the numbers for your quantitative analysis. You're more likely to make a mistake if you rush; so, make sure you slow down.

Basic Structure of the Non-Case Part of the Interview

The interpersonal, or get-to-know-you part of the case interview will likely either be divided into two 15-minute portions by two different interviewers and tacked onto the case portion of the interview, or it will be given a full 30- to 45-minute interview by one interviewer. Either way, you should plan for at least 30 minutes of interpersonal interviewing—and if you do have two interviewers, be sure that you tell them different stories, as they will confer with each other later, and you don't want to look like you just had the same conversation twice!

30- to 45-minute "Get to know you"

The get-to-know-you part of the interview is structured the same way as all other interpersonal interviews. It generally consists of the following parts:

1) A resume walk, where the interviewer asks how the interviewee's previous experience has led him or her to this point

2) A few interpersonal/personal quality questions, where the interviewee tells a story that demonstrates his or her answer to the question.

3) A few minutes at the end for the interviewee to ask the interviewer questions.

A full list of questions that you can expect—and follow-up questions for firms that really "drill-down" on interpersonal stories and questions—is included in an appendix.

What they're testing

Generally, firms are looking for interviewees to show structured thinking, creative thinking, ability to synthesize, problem-solving skills, good teamwork and leadership skills in the get-to-know you interview. You'll recognize many of these things as the same skills that they're testing for in the case interview itself. Interviewees that do really well in the interpersonal interview structure their interpersonal answers ("The three key learnings from starting a new organization in college for me were: one …"), synthesize their answers effectively by keeping all stories to under three to five minutes, and choose stories that fit with the values of the firm and the profession.

Leadership and achievement

Most firms want to hire top talent and are, therefore, looking for candidates with a clear track record of substantive leadership and achievement. Firms want consultants who will work late, go the extra mile and overachieve for the clients that are spending so much money on their services. So, be sure to demonstrate your overachievement in your stories. Don't just list off titles in clubs—instead, pick one club or activity where you rose through the ranks, were dedicated and pulled a couple all-nighters, because that's the kind of consultant they want for their team.

Personality

Interviewers are evaluating your personality on two dimensions: 1) would I trust this person to deal effectively with my clients?, and 2) do I want to be stuck in an airport with this person? This is a two-pronged personality test that, some might argue, asks you to wear two very different hats at once. Without being completely contradictory, this means you need to do the following balancing act in your get-to-know-you conversation: show that you can be serious and relate to CEOs, while also showing that you have a bit of a fun-loving side; be appropriate in all of your comments, while also showing that you can laugh at a few jokes over dinner. In other words, have some personality, without having too much personality. It's a fine line to walk, but that's part of what they're looking for in this part of the interview.

Fit with the firm/interest in the firm

Each firm has its own set of values, and while many of these values and cultural attributes overlap with those of other firms, they do like to think of themselves as different from each other. Because of this, you should do your own homework on the firms to try to discover their little difference and see which

    © 2008 Vault.com Inc.

fits your personality the best. Then show off your knowledge to your interviewers—show that you've done your homework; make it clear that you're dedicated and committed to only working at their firm. It will not only show your interviewers that you have a particular interest in their firm, but it will also make them feel like they work at everyone's favorite firm.

Do's and Don'ts of the Non-Case Part of the Interview

Besides the specific personal qualities, interpersonal skills, and achievements that they're looking for you to mention in the get-to-know-you part of the interview, there are a few tips that will help you to show just how personable a person and overall, well-rounded a consultant you can be. The following are some "Do's and Don'ts" to keep in mind about the non-case part of the interview, which will reinforce your demonstrated consulting skills from the case interview.

Do's

Do try "to tell a story."

People remember stories. They remember a concise beginning, middle and end. You want your answers to be quick, interesting, insightful little stories that they will remember and be able to tell later in the day when they're with all the other interviewers sorting through candidates and deciding which interviewees will get the job. Furthermore, consultants often think of their presentations to clients as stories of analysis that lead to a given recommendation, and are looking for your ability to tell stories concisely and effectively in this part of the interview.

Do have questions to ask.

Most all interviewers leave at least five minutes of time at the end of the interview for questions—in many ways, it's interviewer etiquette to do so. So don't disappoint them by having nothing to ask. Your interviewers want to see that you're a curious, inquisitive person; your interviewers also want to see that you can do both sides of a conversation. Furthermore, your interviewers likely just spent a good amount of time asking you questions about you—it would seem a bit self-absorbed if you had nothing to ask them back. So, prepare a couple questions about the firm, about how they chose consulting as a career, about their recent casework—they don't have to be the most insightful questions in the world. You just need to ask something—and hopefully, if you really are interested in having a job like the one your interviewers have, your questions will be sincere, too.

Don'ts

Don't forget to answer the actual question first!

Often, interviewers will ask very pointed questions like: "What are your biggest weaknesses?" and interviewees will launch on to their practiced, prepared story that shows their weakness but how they're working on it and never answer the question first. Be sure to answer the question. Sure, have your five to seven stories that show your personal qualities and achievements practiced and ready for this part of the interview. But please be sure to answer the question at hand first, and to make a clear transition to your story. The interviewers actually do want their questions answered and a clear answer is required.

Don't forget to be structured, clear, and concise in your answers.

Have you ever heard the joke about one consultant asking another what his plans were on a Friday night? The second consultant answers: "Well, for this Friday, I can think of three options: 1) go to a movie, 2) go to dinner, or 3) go to dinner and a movie." There are very simple ways that you can make all of your answers very structured and clear—regardless of what the question is. While this is the interpersonal part of the interview, you should constantly try to reinforce your innate and pervasive use of structured thinking in your answers to questions here.

Practicing Interviewing

Practicing cases, practicing math

Practicing cases will not only make you more comfortable with cases, it will actually make you better at them. The more of them that you work through, the more types of cases, industries, businesses and business problems you'll see, and you'll become an expert at cases. In the way that consultants get better at being consultants the more cases that they do, you'll become better at case interviewing the more you practice.

And in terms of specifically how to practice cases, don't practice them by yourself. If you really do want to simulate the case interview experience to its

© 2008 Vault.com Inc.

fullest, have someone else play the interviewer and give you the cases. Even better, have someone that you don't know that well play your interviewer. If you only practice cases with your best friends with whom you're likely very comfortable, you won't simulate the experience of having a case interviewer you don't know well giving you cases.

Finally, another good thing to practice is your elementary school math. Most people preparing for interviews have not done math without a calculator since third grade; so, your skills of doing math with pen and paper are likely a little rusty. The best remedy is to take out a pen and white paper and practice a little old-fashioned multiplication and long division for a few hours one afternoon. You'll find that it's like riding a bicycle, but you'll be happy you got back on the bicycle before your interview day.

Practicing "non-case" part of interviews

You will spend a majority of your time practicing case interviews—and this is probably where you should spend a majority of your time. However, if you haven't interviewed in a while (case interviewed or otherwise), it's recommended that you spend some time practicing the non-case part of case interviews as well. Everyone can get a little rusty and would benefit from a little warming up before going back into the interviewing world. Furthermore, because the non-case part of a case interview is supposed to reinforce many of the skills shown in the case, it's advisable to practice this part, too, as a solid get-to-know-you interview can make or break your chances for the next round of a top-tier consulting interview. (Remember: They're evaluating you for what you'll look like in front of a client, as much as your Excel or data analysis skills.)

Visit the Vault Consulting Career Channel at **www.vault.com/consulting** — with insider firm profiles, message boards, the Vault Consulting Job Board and more.

VAULT CAREER LIBRARY   **11**

Case Interview Categories

Guesstimates/brainteasers

These are short math problems that some consulting firms use, instead of a case, in order to assess an applicant's quantitative abilities, structured thinking and creativity with data. They tend to be rather silly "sizing" questions, but they're a good way to practice the thinking skills that you need to be fluent in the case without having to practice a whole case. (An appendix of examples of these types of questions is included on page 177.)

Market sizing

A market sizing case may be as simple as many guesstimates that you've seen and practiced, but it is a typical consulting exercise in many consulting cases. Often, these cases will ask you to do a few things: 1) propose numerous ways in which to size the market, 2) size the actual market in one or two of those ways, and account for why the answers are different and which answer might be better, and 3) make an estimate on how that market might grow/decline in the near future. Sometimes, a market sizing case will involve estimating what a client's penetration of that market is as well.

For more advanced case interviewees (a former consultant or banker, or an MBA graduate), a market sizing will be just the first step of a much larger case, such as a new product/market entry case or an acquisition case. However, for a more junior candidate (an undergraduate, or someone with little business background), a market sizing exercise might be the entire meat of the case interview.

Industry analysis

Industry analysis is another very common case interview, or just a common part of a larger case. Porter's Five Forces or the three Cs (company, competitors, customers) are the most common frameworks used to approach an industry analysis case. And while you should definitely be able to work through any industry analysis without any specific knowledge of that industry, a little thought as to what might drive that industry (R&D and marketing for pharma/biotech, costs for the manufacturing sector, risk and financing for a finance company) will also be of use as you work through the case. Because of this, it's always good to be reading the business section of the newspaper or *The Wall Street Journal* for the weeks before your case interviews so that you have

   © 2008 Vault.com Inc.

a little more general business sense before you're confronted with a bunch of business problems in your case interviews.

Profitability

This is likely the most commonly practiced type of case interview, as it has the easiest framework at the beginning. This case usually begins: "Our client is facing declining profitability, and they've come to us to help them figure out why." The easiest framework to apply to this is: Profits = Revenue - Costs. After that, you only need to make a quick hypothesis as to which side might be driving the profit loss—or ask your interviewer, or flip a coin—and then you're off down the path of either volume multiplied by price, or COGs, and a series of questions to your interviewer to get more data. Profitability cases are good to practice to get comfortable structuring a case, asking questions to get data, etc., but they are rarely seen in consulting in practice (and are therefore used less in an interview). So, after you've practiced a few of these and become comfortable, be sure to get comfortable with other types of cases and case questions.

Acquisition/valuation

This type of case will likely only be given to candidates with backgrounds in finance, those with business degrees, or interviewees applying to corporate finance practices at firms. Getting comfortable with discounting cash flows simply (using a 10 percent rate over 10 years) is likely the hurdle to these cases. Other than that, a simple industry analysis will likely be the only additional step before making a recommendation at the end of the case.

New product/market entry

This is a very typical case interview (and real-life consulting case). It usually combines a little market sizing analysis, a little industry analysis, and either an acquisition/valuation or a marketing framework and idea generation at the end. Because it combines so many frameworks and types of analysis, it's a great type of case interview to practice.

Operations

While operations cases tend to be few and far between, some consulting firms specialize in operations and supply chain management; so, if you're applying to such a firm, it's good to practice at least a few operations cases.

Visit the Vault Consulting Career Channel at **www.vault.com/consulting** — with insider firm profiles, message boards, the Vault Consulting Job Board and more.

VAULT CAREER LIBRARY

13

The case they are working on or just finished

Often, case interviewers will create a case on the spot about the case that they are currently working on, or have just finished. They will usually inform you of that. If this happens, try to approach the case with the same sort of structured thinking and approach that you would any other case interview, but view the case interview as a conversation and ask more questions. Maybe you would add a dose more of humility to the entire affair. Likely, the interviewers have more of an opinion about what the right answer is in this case and the best way to approach the problem—more than they would in a case that they did not handle themselves—so, you should try to discern their answer. This does not mean that you should abandon all the great case interviewing skills that you have practiced, but you should recognize that your interviewers may have a bit more "skin in the game" on this one. So, pay close attention to their hints, be more flexible in redirecting the course that you take and make sure that you're fully engaging them, as they really are "the expert" here and you should treat them as such. If you really want to score bonus points at the end of one of these types of case interviews, ask your interviewers how the project ended, what the client thought, or if there was any follow-up casework because of their work here.

(Note: The cool thing about this type of case is that you get a real-life window view into the world of consulting: you get to see an actual case and its answer. Often, they'll show you actual data. It's a good way to see if you're actually interested in the work of a consultant, and it can be a great forum to really engage your interviewers and show off your soft skills of creativity, flexibility and curiosity in the case interview setting.)

© 2008 Vault.com Inc.

A Note on Categorizing

It's important to note that a large percentage of consulting cases you'll come across, including many in this guide, do not fall neatly into one category. In fact, some cases incorporate two or more of the aforementioned categories, such as a profitability case that includes market sizing. While it's good to familiarize yourself with all of these kinds of cases, be prepared for a case that asks you to tackle a blend of frameworks. And beware of too readily pigeonholing a case as one distinct category—it may be a red herring planted by your interviewer.

Finally, there are some seasoned consultants who believe that certain leading firms tend to stick to a distinctive interviewing style. For example, a BCG case interview may require an interviewee to be particularly proactive in seeking relevant data, often given verbally, and then make quick back-of-envelope calculations (e.g. PetCo case, page 132). A Bain interview may require the interviewee to derive insights from a series of slides, as in the Eyewear Chain case, page 62. And at McKinsey, an interviewer may push the candidate to answer more and more specific questions as the case interview progresses, testing creativity and the ability to generate new ideas (e.g. Pro Bono case, page 136). At Monitor, a typical first round may involve 20 to 25 minutes of reviewing a two- to three-page case and several charts to answer three questions, one of which is quantitative while the others are qualitative. Examples of these are the Amusement Park case and the Organic Fast-Food Chain case. However, it should go without saying that interviewees should be ready to expect anything; there are plenty of consultants who insist that there is no clear distinction between interviewing styles at specific firms.

Visit the Vault Consulting Career Channel at www.vault.com/consulting — with insider firm profiles, message boards, the Vault Consulting Job Board and more.

VAULT CAREER LIBRARY   15

VΛULT

THE MOST TRUSTED NAME IN CAREER INFORMATION

Vault guides and employer profiles have been published since 1997 and are the premier source of insider information on careers.

Each year, Vault surveys and interviews thousands of employees to give readers the inside scoop on industries and specific employers to help them get the jobs they want.

"Fun reads, edgy details"
– FORBES MAGAZINE

"To get the unvarnished scoop, check out Vault"
– SMARTMONEY MAGAZINE

VΛULT

SAMPLE
CASES

VAULT CAREER LIBRARY

© 2008 Vault.com Inc.

Amusement Park Case

Please read the following situation carefully and answer the three questions. You may use the calculator, paper and pen made available to you. After 20 minutes, you will walk through your solutions with the consultant.

Situation

You are the business development director for a nationwide theme park called "Thrilly" specializing in thrill rides and targeting kids from age eight to 16. Thrilly has over 18 theme parks all over the United States. One of your tasks is to determine where to site the latest theme park. After a year of assessment, your team has determined three suitable areas for future consideration. These are locations A, B and C. These areas are free of competition from similar theme parks in a two-hour driving radius. In situating a theme park, there are major cost considerations, and determining the future revenue potential is critical to ensuring that the project site will bring in the greatest positive net outcome for Thrilly. Your experiences have taught you not to underestimate the effort and time spent on determining the right site. The last business development director was fired for making a less optimal decision, and you vowed not to repeat the same mistake.

Your experienced team has provided you with a lot of information, and some pieces will definitely be more relevant than others. You decide to shift through all the analyzed information in a single setting to develop an initial hypothesis as to which is the most profitable site, before moving forward to recheck the data gathering and analysis process. Therefore, at this stage of analysis, it is important to consider the most important cost and revenue components, rather than getting mired in the details.

Cost of theme park development

One of the main costs for the development of a theme park is leasing the land. Theme parks do not buy the land outright because of the risk in selling off such a large piece of land in the future if the theme park is closed down.

After leasing the land, the cost of building the theme park is entirely driven by the time taken to build the theme park. Therefore, labor costs are the main variable component. Your team has painstakingly projected that it will require 400 days for a team of 100 workers to construct and set up the theme park in any of the three locations.

The cost of acquiring, transporting and setting up the actual rides will be the same regardless of the location, so this should not be a factor in the cost-benefit analysis.

After the theme park is built, it will be critical to consider the operating cost of the theme park. The operating cost will only be affected by the number of days it is operating due to weather conditions. During the peak season (summer), the ride frequency is projected to be higher, and therefore resulting in higher operating costs.

Revenue from theme park

To estimate the number of visitors every year, it is important to consider the number of families who will have the disposable income to visit the theme park. The population to be considered lies within a two-hour driving radius around the theme park, as families are unwilling to endure a four-hour drive with their children to and from a theme park.

Thrilly classified the relevant population under three socioeconomic statuses. Families under status C will not visit Thrilly due to their lack of disposable income. On the average, families under status B will visit Thrilly once every two years, and families with the highest socioeconomic status (A) will visit Thrilly once every year. Families' average spending in the theme parks on food and concessions is slightly different based on their socioeconomic status.

The ticket price for an adult is $40 and the ticket price for a child is $30, regardless of the season.

Other considerations

Beyond the obvious financial calculation, it would be also necessary to evaluate other nonmarket and nonfinancial issues that come with the developing and operating of a theme park. However, your team has not gotten around compiling this information, so you will have to infer the critical issues based on your experiences.

© 2008 Vault.com Inc.

Exhibit 1: Leasing and Labor Cost

Total discounted leasing amount for 15 years ($000)

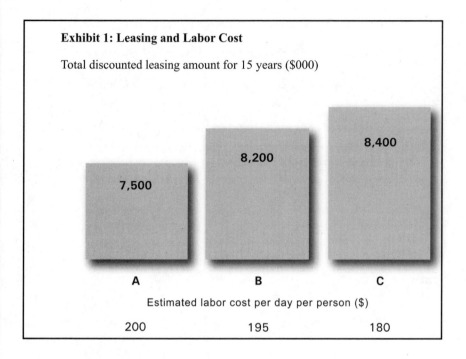

	A	B	C
	7,500	8,200	8,400

Estimated labor cost per day per person ($)

	A	B	C
	200	195	180

Exhibit 2: Weather conditions and operating cost

Number of peak (summer), off-peak (spring and fall) and closed (winter) days

No. of days

	A	B	C
Closed (Winter)	90	80	70
Off-Peak (Spring and Fall)	190	198	200
High Peak (Summer)	85	90	95
	A	B	C

Operating cost per day ($000)

	A	B	C
Low Peak	26	24	26
High Peak	32	33	31

Visit the Vault Consulting Career Channel at **www.vault.com/consulting** — with insider firm profiles, message boards, the Vault Consulting Job Board and more.

VAULT CAREER LIBRARY

21

Exhibit 3: Socioeconomic status of targeted population

Socioeonomic status of population within a two-hour radius of each location

Eligible population willing to visit theme parks

| 350,000 children* | 320,000 visitors | 360,000 visitors |
| 150,000 adults | 180,000 adults | 140,000 adults |

	A	B	C
Status* A	39	25	20
Status B	50	50	60
Status C	20	25	20

% of eligible population*

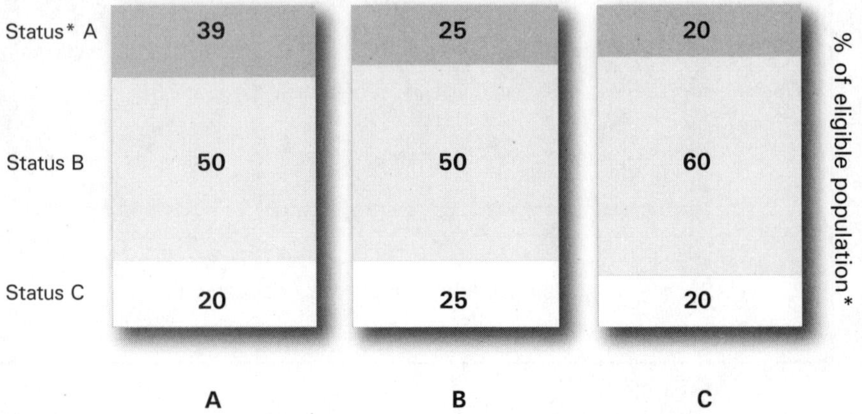

Non-ticket** spend per adult or child based on status ($)

	A	B	C
Status A	10	8	10
Status B	8	6	6

Note: *Assume that the status is evenly distributed as % of addressable population across children and adults*
** *Non-ticket sales consist of average food and concessions spend by each individual (regardless of whether child or adult)*

© 2008 Vault.com Inc.

Questions

Which area will you choose to set up the theme park? Please support your answers with the necessary calculations, using the calculator available to do so.

Cost calculation			
Locations	**A**	**B**	**C**
Building the theme park			
Leasing Cost	$7.5M	$8.2M	$8.4M
Construction costs = Labor cost per day * No. of workers * No. of days of operation	$200 * 100 workers * 400 days = $8M	$195 * 100 * 400 = $7.8M	$180*100 * 400 = $7.2M
Annual operating cost of the park			
Operating costs = Cost per day * days in respective season	$26,000 * 190 + $34,000* 85 =$7.98M	$34,000 *198+$40,000*80 = $7.722M	$32,000 * 200 +$38,000 * 95 = $8.145M

Revenue calculation			
Annual Revenue			
Number of Status A customers who visit each year	350,000*30% = 105,000 children 150,000*30% = 50,000 adults	320,000*25% = 80,000 children 180,000*25%= 45,000 adults	360,000*20% = 72,000 children 140,000*20% = 28,000 adults
Number of Status B customers who visit each year	350,000 * 50%*0.5 = 87,500 children 150,000 * 50%*0.5 = 37,500 adults	320,000*50%*0.5 = 80,000 children 180,000*50%*0.5 = 45,000 adults	360,000*60%*0.5 = 108,000 children 140,000*60%*0.5 = 42,000 adults
Ticket Sales	(105,000 +87,500)*$30 + (50,000+37,500)*$40 = $9.275M	(80,000+80,000) * $30 + (45,000+45,000) * $40 = $8.4M	(72,000+108,000) children *$30 + (28,000+42,000) adults *$40 = $8.2M

Visit the Vault Consulting Career Channel at www.vault.com/consulting — with insider firm profiles, message boards, the Vault Consulting Job Board and more.

VAULT CAREER LIBRARY

23

Final calculation			
Total Building Cost = Lease + Build	$7.5M+$8M = $15.5M	$8.2M+$7.8M = $16M	$8.4M+$7.2M = $15.6M
Total Profit = Revenue – Operating Cost	$12.775M-$7.98M = $4.795M	$10.9M-$7.722M = $3.178	$10M-$8.145M = $1.855

Based on the building cost and net profit, location C will be the most attractive option financially.

What do you think are the top drivers in the net profit of each location, excluding building cost?

Given that the number of adults and children do not differ significantly, one of the key drivers is the socioeconomic status of the population within the two-hour drive, as it determines both the frequency of visits and the amount of non-ticket spends.

The other key driver is the theme park's daily operating costs in each specific location as it directly affects the bottom line.

These two drivers are important levers that affect the net profit for each location.

What are the top nonfinancial or noneconomic considerations to be taken into account when operating the theme park at the area you suggested?

It is critical to manage positive relationships with the surrounding residential clusters by working with local officials to determine how to best manage traffic and noise pollution. Thrilly may have to co-invest in some initiatives to reduce these negative effects. If residents are irritated, then the customer base may shrink, as some residents may boycott the theme park and encourage their neighbors to do so.

Another issue is to continually assure parents about the safety of rides, in the light of accidents in any other theme parks. A major accident in any theme park will adversely affect the number of customers, so it is critical to mitigate the adverse implication of these incidents.

© 2008 Vault.com Inc.

Bicycle Manufacturer Case

Case facts initially offered by the interviewer

• The client is a manufacturer of bicycles and has been in business for 25 years.

• It manufactures and sells three categories of bicycles:

  • Racing bikes: High-end, high-performance bikes for sophisticated cyclists

  • Mainstream bikes: Durable, but not overly complicated bikes for everyday riders

  • Children's bikes: Smaller, simpler versions of its mainstream bikes made for children

• The client profits have been eroding over the past five years.

Questions to be answered by candidate

• What is driving the decline in overall profits?

• What recommendations might correct the situation?

Suggested solutions

To determine what has caused <u>overall</u> profits to decrease the candidate must first understand what has transpired in each of the three product categories over the past five years, during which profitability has slipped. The following are questions and answers that would be provided in an interview scenario.

Interviewee: What is the market size of each of the three segments over the past five years?

Firm: Racing has remained constant at its present size of $300 million. Mainstream has increased at 2 percent growth rate per year to its present size of $1 billion. Children's has increased at 3 percent growth rate per year to its present size of $400 million.

Interviewee: Was there any change in market share in each of these segments over the past five years?

Firm:
Racing market share has decreased from 60 percent to 30 percent.
Mainstream market share has increased from 0 percent to 5 percent.
Children's market share has increased from 0 percent to 3 percent.

Visit the Vault Consulting Career Channel at **www.vault.com/consulting** — with insider firm profiles, message boards, the Vault Consulting Job Board and more.

VAULT CAREER LIBRARY

25

Interviewee: Who are the client's major competitors in each market segment? What has happened to their market share in each segment over the past five years?

Firm: In racing, there is one main competitor and a host of small firms. The main competitor has increased market share from 30 percent to 50 percent. In mainstream, there are many large competitors, none of which holds more than 10 percent of the market. In children's, there are many competitors, none with more than 10 percent of the market.

Interviewee: Can I have the details of your client's margins for a bicycle in each of the three segments?

Firm:
Racing: Cost = $600/unit, Profit = $300/unit
Mainstream: Cost = $250/unit, Profit = $75/unit
Children's: Cost = $200/unit, Profit = $50/unit

Interviewee: What is the client's costing policy?

Firm: The client has a single manufacturing and assembly plant. It has separate lines in this facility to produce racing, mainstream and children's products. The costs are divided into three categories: labor, material and overhead.

Interviewee: Do we have the current breakdown of costs along these categories for each product segment?

Firm:
Racing: Labor = 30 percent, Material = 40 percent, Overhead = 30 percent
Mainstream: Labor = 25 percent, Material = 40 percent, Overhead = 35 percent
Children's: Labor = 25 percent, Material = 40 percent, Overhead = 35 percent

Interviewee: Has there been any increase in costs over the year? Has the mix of expenses changed over the past five years?

Firm: Overall costs have been increasing at a fairly hefty rate of 10 percent per year. In all segments, labor is an increasing percentage of the costs.

The above information should be used by the candidate to analyze the following scenario:

• The client, with a commanding position in a flat market segment (racing), expanded into new segments (mainstream and children's). This move has seemingly created an unfavorable mix, thus decreasing the market share in the most lucrative segment (racing).

• The decline in profits can be deduced as follows:

© 2008 Vault.com Inc.

Profits five years ago = $60 million (=60 percent x $300 million x 33 percent racing margin)

Profits today = $44 million (=(30 percent x $300 million x 33 percent racing margin) + (5 percent x $1 billion x 23 percent mainstream margin) + (3 percent x $400 million x 20 percent children's margin).

To understand the dramatic decrease in market share in the racing segment, the following questions can be asked for further probing:

Interviewee: Have there been any major changes in product quality or price in your client's racing product? Or in its main competitor's racing product?

Firm: No.

Interviewee: What is the current distribution network for the client's products?

Firm:
Racing: Small specialty dealers, mass distributors and discount stores
Mainstream: Mass distributors and discount stores
Children's: Mass distributors and discount stores

Interviewee: Have any significant changes taken place in the distribution network for your client's racing product? Or for its main competitor's racing product?

Firm: Yes. Previously the client and its main competitor in the racing segment sold exclusively through small, specialty dealers. This remains unchanged for the competition. However, the client also began to use the distribution network of mainstream and children's bikes for its racing bikes.

Interviewee: Is the pricing policy of the mass distributors and discount stores different from the specialty stores for racing bikes?

Firm: Prices at these stores tend to be 15 to 20 percent less.

Interviewee: After the change in distribution network, what percent of the client's racing sales occurs in mass distributors and discount stores?

Firm: Effectively none. The attempt to sell through these distributors seems to have failed.

Interviewee: Has there been any recent study on brand image of the client's racing product, especially after it altered its distribution network?

Firm: No studies have been done.

Interviewee: Any significant change in the client's relationship with the specialty outlets after the new distribution network was adopted?

Firm: Again, no formal analysis has been performed.

The next step

Although some analysis and/or survey should be performed to answer the last two questions more conclusively, a possible analysis can be derived.

• There has been no significant change in either quality or price (or any other tangible factor) of the client's racing product relative to its competition. It is not the product that is the problem, but rather its image.

• As your client introduced lower end (mainstream and children's) products and began to push its racing bike segment sales through mass distributors and discount outlets, its reputation seemed to have been compromised.

• In addition, the presence of the racing products in the discount outlets has put your historic racing distributor (the specialty shops) in a precarious position. The specialty shops need to now lower the price to compete with the other networks of the racing segment, thereby cutting their own profits. Instead, they might be tempted to push the competition's product. Especially since the client has no direct sales force at the retail outlets and the specialty shops essentially serve as the client's sales force.

It is also known from the initial discussion that labor costs have been increasing over the years. Further questions to uncover cost issues would include:

Interviewee: Is the workforce unionized?

Firm: Yes.

Interviewee: What is the average age of the workforce?

Firm: Fifty-two and climbing. There is very little turnover in the workforce.

Interviewee: What is the present throughput rating? How has it changed over the past five years?

Firm: Presently the plant is producing at about 80 percent of capacity. This has been decreasing steadily over the last several years.

Interviewee: Are there many instances of equipment shutdowns?

Firm: Yes.

Interviewee: What is the typical reason for equipment shutdown?

Firm: Emergency repair.

Interviewee: Describe the preventive maintenance program in effect at the client's facility?

Firm: Preventive maintenance is performed informally based on the knowledge of senior technicians.

Interviewee: How often has equipment been replaced? Is this consistent with the original equipment manufacturer's recommendations?

Firm: The client feels that most OEM recommendations are very conservative. It has followed a philosophy of maximizing the life of its equipment and has generally doubled OEM recommendations.

Interviewee: Does the basic approach to manufacturing (i.e., the mix of labor and technology) reflect that of its competition?

Firm: The client tells you that there is a continuing movement to automate and utilize technology to improve efficiency throughout the industry, but it is his/her opinion that his/her approach, maintaining the "human touch," is what differentiates them from the competition. (Unfortunately, he or she is right!)

Possible approaches

The above information is sufficient to add some understanding to the cost side of the equation and why labor costs have been on the rise.

- The client has an aging workforce and the plant lags behind in terms of technology and innovation. This has contributed to excessive breakdowns, decreased throughput, increased labor rates (wages increase with seniority) and greater labor hours (overtime to fix broken machines).

In proposing recommendations to improve the client's situation, there is no single correct approach. There are a number of approaches that might be explored and recommended. The following are some possibilities:

- Abandon the mainstream and children's segment to recover leadership in the lucrative and more profitable racing segment.

Issues to consider in this approach:

- How much of the racing segment is recoverable?
- What are the expected growth rates of each segment?
- How badly damaged is the relationship with the specialty outlets?
- Are there alternative outlets to the specialty shops, such as Internet sales?
- How will this move affect overall utilization of the operating facilities?

• Maintain the mainstream and children's segments, but sell these under a different name. This will maintain the brand image of the racing segment. Revert to the specialty outlets for racing segment.

Issues to consider in this approach:

  • Is there demand among the mass and discount distributors for bicycles under the client's name?
  • What is the relationship status with the specialty outlets?
  • What additional advertising and promotional costs might be incurred?
  • What are the expected growth rates for each segment?
  • What is driving the buying habits of the mainstream and children's market?

• Reduce costs through automation and innovation.

Issues to be considered:

  • What technological improvements are to be made?
  • What are the required investments?
  • What are the expected returns on those investments?
  • How will these investments affect throughput?
  • To which lines are these investments appropriate?
  • Are the mainstream and children's segments potentially "over-engineered?"
  • What impact will this have on the required workforce levels?
  • If layoffs are required to achieve the benefits, what impact will this have on labor relations?

• Reduce costs through establishing a formal preventive maintenance program.

Issues to be considered:

  • What organizational changes will be required?
  • What analysis will be performed to determine the appropriate amount of PM?
  • What training is required of the workforce?
  • What technical or system changes are required?
  • How will the unionized workforce respond?

Key takeaways

This case can be lengthy and very involved. It is not expected that a candidate would cover all of the above topics, but rather work through selected topics in a logical fashion. It is important that the candidate pursue a solution that considers both revenue and cost issues and how these impact profit. Additionally, a candidate's ability to work comfortably with the quantitative side of this case

© 2008 Vault.com Inc.

is important. The above recommendations for improving profitability are just a few among many. The candidate may come up with his or her own ideas.

B2B Fertilizer Manufacturer Case

A large farm equipment manufacturer and distributor is our client. It is considering whether or not it should buy a B2B fertilizer company. This case has two main questions: 1) Should our client buy the company?, and 2) How would you value how much that fertilizer company is worth to our client?

Additional information provided during questioning

• The client is a large farm equipment manufacturer and distributor based in the U.S., but it has operations overseas as well.

• The client serves both the B2B market and B2C market, but the B2C market has been dwindling in terms of farm equipment, as mom-and-pop farming in the U.S. has declined significantly over the last few decades. However, the B2C market has grown in terms of home gardening equipment, which our client has exploited for its lighter equipment and product lines.

• The acquisition target company is a midsized fertilizer company, which markets its products in the B2B market. It has a 35 percent market share in the farming industry, which it achieved because that industry has consolidated over the last few decades. It sells its products only in the U.S. This is a standard acquisition case that requires structuring and analysis of two main parts in order to complete:

1) A standard three Cs analysis of whether or not this is a smart acquisition for the client given market conditions.

2) Valuation of the fertilizer company, both as a stand-alone unit and with the revenue and cost synergies that could be achieved with the client.

Breakdown of solution

Interviewee: Let me just make sure I understand the case.

Firm: Sure.

Interviewee: So, the client is a large farm equipment manufacturer and distributor, and it's thinking of buying a fertilizer company. It's hired us to tell it whether or not that's the right thing to do strategically, and to tell it how much it should purchase the company for.

Firm: That's right. Do you have any questions before we get started?

Interviewee: Actually, can I know a little more about the client?

Firm: Sure. The client is a large farm equipment manufacturer and distributor based in the U.S., but it has operations overseas as well. The client serves both the B2B market and B2C market, but the B2C market has been dwindling in terms of farm equipment, as mom-and-pop farming in the U.S. has declined significantly over the last few decades. However, the B2C market has grown in terms of home gardening equipment, which our client has exploited for its lighter equipment and product lines.

Interviewee: That's great. And is the target also a B2B and B2C manufacturer and supplier?

Firm: Actually, it's not. The acquisition target is a midsized fertilizer company that markets its products in the B2B market. It has a 35 percent market share in the farming industry, which it achieved because that industry has consolidated over the last few decades. It sells its products only in the U.S. Is that enough info for you to get started?

Interviewee: Yes. That's great. Can I have a few minutes to collect my thoughts?

Firm: Of course. Take your time. Just let me know when you're ready.

(A few minutes go by …)

Interviewee: I would divide my analysis into whether or not it should even buy the company into three main questions:

1) What would this acquisition do for the company's brand, core capabilities, product line offering, operations, and short- and long-term market strategy?

2) What would this acquisition do for the client's customer base? Will a fertilizer base grow the client's customer base or the amount current customers spend with us?

3) What would this acquisition do for the client's competitive outlook? Is this a necessary acquisition given the competition, or will this give the client a competitive advantage over the competition?

An experienced interviewee could organize his thoughts and questions in a table like the one below.

COMPANY
- Will this acquisition add to the client's current portfolio of products?
- Will this acquisition add to the client's capabilities
- Does the acquisition add to the client's corporate brand? Or does it detract for some reason?
- How long will it take to fully intergrate the acquisition? WIll this detract from any currently pressing matters for the client?
- Is the acquisition affordable to the client right now? How will the acquisition be financed?

CUSTOMERS
- Will the acquisition add to the client's current base? Or are there redundancies in the two company's customer bases?
- Does the acquisition detract from the client's current customer base for any reason

COMPETITORS
- How will the competition react to this acquisition?
- Will this acquisition give the client a competitive advantage in the market?
- Is it a competitive necessity to make this acquisition? What kinds of business lines do competitors have that the client does not?

Visit the Vault Consulting Career Channel at **www.vault.com/consulting** — with insider firm profiles, message boards, the Vault Consulting Job Board and more.

VAULT CAREER LIBRARY 33

Firm: That's great. That's kind of how we approached the case. Given what you know about the client and the acquisition, do you have any answers, or even hypotheses, that answer some of those questions?

Interviewee: Well, in terms of the company, its capabilities and its brand, it seems like the acquisition would add to its capabilities. The client makes farm equipment and the target makes fertilizer. So, the acquisition would add to its product line and capabilities.

Firm: That's right. What about in terms of customers?

Interviewee: Well, if I remember correctly, you said that the client is both a B2B player and a B2C player, whereas the fertilizer company is only a B2B player. So, I doubt that the acquisition would really grow the client's customer base significantly in the consumer market. However, you also mentioned that the fertilizer company had achieved a 35 percent market share in the B2B market—that's a pretty good share. If our client doesn't have that with its farming business customers, maybe owning the target can help it get there. Also, maybe the client can start to sell more—that is, cross sell fertilizer—to its consumer base if it buys this fertilizer company.

Firm: That's right. That's one of the main reasons it was considering this acquisition—for the cross-selling opportunities. What about in terms of competition?

(Here, the interviewer is testing two things: 1) An interviewee's ability to pay attention, take good notes and review them quickly, and 2) An interviewee's ability to say/admit when he/she doesn't know something—consultants often have to admit what they don't know to their industry-expert clients; so, it is often a skill tested for in interviews.)

Interviewee: Um, well, unless I missed something, I'm not sure I know much about the competitive environment. I know that the fertilizer company is doing well in the fertilizer market with a 35 percent share, but I don't think I know how well our client is doing in the farm equipment market—or the consumer market.

Firm: Actually, you don't know much now. Let's get into that a bit. There are only two other competitors in the farm equipment market, and with the farming industry consolidating, competition has gotten fierce. The client has begun to turn increasingly to its consumer business for its growth. It likes this acquisition both because it might help it get a slight edge over its competition in its B2B space and because it might help it grow its consumer business with an expanded product line.

Interviewee: Well, that certainly explains things.

Firm: Now, what about the second question from the client?

© 2008 Vault.com Inc.

Interviewee: Oh, right, how much should it pay for this acquisition?

Firm: Yes. How would you go about structuring that part of the case? Go ahead and take a few minutes if you need it.

(Few minutes go by ...)

Interviewee: It seems like there are three pieces of value for the client: 1) The value of the fertilizer company as a stand-alone division, 2) The value of any cost synergies that there might exist between the client and the acquisition, and 3) The value of the revenue synergies that the client could get from the acquisition—that's the cross-selling opportunities that we were talking about earlier. If you total that up, that's the maximum price that the client should pay for the acquisition.

(The relationship between the pieces of value are illustrated in the table on page 36.)

Firm: That's perfect. Now, which of those synergies are the most difficult to achieve—or longest term?

(This is an advanced question—probably not appropriate for undergrad case interviewees, but very appropriate for business school interviewees.)

Interviewee: Well, cost synergies are easiest to achieve—if there are two sales people calling on the same farm customer, it's easy to just cut one out without hurting the business. I mean, it may be painful for the business—it's never fun to lay people off, but cost synergies are easy to see and achieve.

It's revenue synergies that are more uncertain. It takes longer to get new products into the sales cycle, and then, you're never sure that your customers will buy your new products.

Firm: That's perfect.

Visit the Vault Consulting Career Channel at www.vault.com/consulting — with insider firm profiles, message boards, the Vault Consulting Job Board and more.

VAULT CAREER LIBRARY 35

VALUE OF THE COMPANY AS A STAND-ALONE UNIT	+	VALUE OF THE COMPANY AS A STAND-ALONE UNIT	+	VALUE OF THE COMPANY AS A STAND-ALONE UNIT

- Net present value of the profits of the acquisition for some appropriate time period into the future

- Overlap in overhead/ headquarters/general expenses
- Overlap in manufacturing/operations
- Overlap in sales force/marketing/corporate branding

Cost-cutting, more easily achieved synergies

- Cross-selling opportunities of farm equipment products of the client to B2B customers of acquisition
- Cross-selling opportunities of fertilizer products to client' consumer and business customers

Riskier synergies— more difficult to achieve, longer term

Firm: Now, let's look at those revenue synergies a little more closely. We know that our client sells its light farm equipment to three national home improvement chains in the U.S. as a part of its B2C business. We've done some research on these three retailers and determined that they are selling $15 million each in fertilizer to consumers. Retailer margin on fertilizer is about 10 percent. If we think the client can capture 25 percent of the fertilizer sales to these three national retailers, how much is that worth to us in revenue?

Interviewee: Well, if there are three retailers, and each is selling $15 million in fertilizer, then they're selling $45 million total. If retailers have a 10 percent markup on fertilizer, then that means that the value of those sales to the manufacturer is $40.5 million (10 percent of $45 million is 4.5 million; $45-4.5 = $40.5 million). If we think that we can capture 25 percent, that means we can capture a little over $10 million in B2C revenue synergies.

Firm: That's great. Now, let's pretend that you've just run into the head of corporate development and strategy at the client site. He's anxious to hear about whether or not we think this acquisition is a good idea—what would you say?

Interviewee: I would say that we believe that the acquisition is a good idea, primarily because it will help bolster the company's offering to farming business customers, who are becoming a tougher segment to win, and because it will allow us to really grow our consumer offering, which needs to be an area of high growth for the company. In fact, if we can achieve a 25 percent share of the fertilizer sales at three national retailers, we'll see $10 million in revenue synergies from the acquisition alone, which would be great growth for that side of the business.

(It's important that the interviewee use any quantitative analysis done during the case interview in his or her summary—it shows that the interviewee recognizes how important the bottom line is, and it wraps up the case nicely.)

Firm: That's great. We're done here.

Chinese Chemical Market Case

Your client is an Argentinean chemical conglomerate that produces a wide range of chemicals. The CEO of one of the divisions is concerned about the increasing production of chemical X in China. Specifically, he is concerned about the import of chemical X into Brazil, which will threaten the company's dominant domestic market position, and the company's primary export market, which is the U.S. In addition, the CEO is also interested in entering the China market to produce chemical X to take advantage of the low labor and material cost. How will you approach this problem?

Interviewee: The client is concerned about China's threat to the company's domestic and export markets, and also whether it makes sense to produce chemical X in China. I would like to take a step back to understand which of the three concerns is the most important?

Firm: Unfortunately, its revenue for chemical X is evenly split between the domestic and export market, and the company has always been wondering whether it should enter China. The CEO wants a plan to approach all three problems.

Interviewee: It is unfortunate we cannot prioritize our approach, so I will focus on the three concerns equally.

Firm: Correct. Let's focus on the first concern. How will you determine if his domestic position will be threatened by China's production of chemical X?

Interviewee: I would like to benchmark the client's cost structure of producing chemical X with the more efficient and larger Chinese chemical X producers. The cost of producing any chemical should be distributed between labor, raw materials and overhead such as the manufacturing plant. In addition, there will be transportation costs and even tariffs for the Chinese produced chemical X if it is exported into Argentina. Unless the labor and raw material cost in China are significantly cheaper, my initial hypothesis is that Chinese produced chemical X will not be a threat to the client's domestic market.

Firm: That's a reasonable hypothesis. Why do you think that Chinese labor and raw material cost are comparable to the client?

Interviewee: In Argentina, I believe the client can obtain cost-competitive skilled labor as compared to China, and sourcing for raw materials throughout South America should be reasonably as cost efficient as in China.

Firm: Okay. Let's move on to the second concern. How will you further determine if Chinese producer will threaten the client's primary export market in the U.S. since both of them are exporting their products?

Interviewee: I will assess the amount and growth of exports out of China for chemical X. Given the strong economic growth of China, I will assume that domestic demand is also increasing. Therefore, the amount and growth of exports will be driven by how much domestic production exceeds domestic demand, and this insight can also help to answer the third concern.

Firm: How will you assess the production level in China?

Interviewee: Given the lack of high-quality market data in China, it is critical to look into different data sources to triangulate the result.

First, I will buy research reports from multiple local private market research companies in China who actually track both the production size and growth of chemical X from state-owned enterprises and private enterprises.

Second, I will interview the head of the chemical X association in China to cross-check the data on these market research reports.

Third, I will interview relevant senior managers of the top three to five largest private sector companies about the overall production level of chemical X and its growth rate in China. I do not think the senior management team from the Chinese state-owned enterprise will speak to an international management consultancy, even on the overall chemical production level and the projected growth rate.

© 2008 Vault.com Inc.

Firm: That seems to be reasonable. How do you plan to assess the domestic demand level in China?

Interviewee: In order to assess the domestic demand, it is important to assess the downstream demand for chemical X. Can I find out what products will need chemical X?

Firm: Let's assume there are only three products that will need chemical X. Take the example of one of the three products. How will you estimate the demand and growth of this product?

Interviewee: I will actually employ the same process as determining the production of chemical X by using the local market research firm, talking to the association for the product and interview the relevant management of the top producers to determine the market size and growth of the product. An additional step will be to determine how much per unit of the product will require chemical X and extrapolate accordingly. It is also important to determine if there will be a substitute to chemical X for the product and the rate of substitution.

Firm: Can you calculate for me the demand for chemical X for the current year and next year based on this table, assuming no substitution for chemical X?

Products	Units (M)	Per unit usage of Chemical X for each product	Growth rate Y-o-Y
Product A	15,000	0.2	3%
Product B	10,000	0.1	5%
Product C	20,000	0.35	10%

Interviewee: The current demand will be sum of the usage of chemical X by these three products, which will be $15,000*0.2+10,000*0.1+20,000*0.35 = 3,000+1,000+7,000 = 11,000$ of chemical X.

The demand for next year will be $3,000*(1.03)+1,000*(1.05)+7,000*(1.1) = 3,090+1,050+7,700 = 11,840$ units of chemical X.

Firm: Thanks for walking me through your calculations. What is the percentage increase for the Chinese domestic demand of chemical X?

Interviewee: It is $(11,840-11000)/11,000 = 7.6$ percent increase. This is a fairly aggressive growth rate.

Visit the Vault Consulting Career Channel at www.vault.com/consulting — with insider firm profiles, message boards, the Vault Consulting Job Board and more.

VAULT CAREER LIBRARY   39

Firm: Okay. What's next?

Interviewee: Once we have an estimated market size and growth for the relevant products for chemical X, we will be able to assess the domestic demand and the demand growth rate for chemical X. We need to verify the reasonable assumption that the producers in China who need chemical X will first purchase it domestically.

Firm: Assume that you have determined both the production and demand of chemical X in China, and found that there will be increasing exports of chemical X in the future, what will be the next step in our analysis?

Interviewee: Let's circle back to the second concern of whether the Chinese producers will threaten the client's primary export market. Assuming their cost structure is relatively competitive and they face the same tariffs, the key differential will be the transportation cost. I will assume the transportation cost will be slightly higher for the Chinese producer than our client because China is further away from the U.S. than Argentina.

Firm: That's a fair assumption. Do you think that is going to make a difference?

Interviewee: I think our client can initially leverage on the cost differentiation. But assuming that the differentiation in transportation cost is minimal, the Chinese exporters of chemical X will definitely pose a threat in the near future.

Firm: What will you advise the client to do then?

Interviewee: The client can work on deepening customer relationships while remaining competitive in price. First, the client can work harder to ensure that its delivery schedule of chemical X meets its U.S. customers' need. Second, the client can better understand the amount of each batch of chemical X that the U.S. customers require, and deliver the exact amount accordingly.

However, given that chemical X appears to be a commoditized chemical, the price differentiation between the Chinese producers and the client should never differ significantly. An effective and deep customer relationship will not overcome a significant price differentiation for a commoditized product. Therefore, the client should definitely look into producing chemical X in China.

Firm: How should we determine if it is a good idea to produce in China, and how should we do so?

Interviewee: Given that we have established that Chinese production has already exceeded Chinese demand, it is unlikely our client will be able to sell to the domestic demand in China if the client went in alone without a Chinese

© 2008 Vault.com Inc.

partner. Another option would be to produce in China for the surrounding export market. It is definitely not a good idea to produce in China to export back into Argentina or South America because of the transportation cost. Therefore, unless circumstance changes and the cost of raw materials or skilled labor in China drop significantly relative to Argentina, I would recommend that our client continue to monitor China's production, but not enter into China right now.

Firm: I agree. Let's assume that the raw material cost has dropped significantly in China as compared to Argentina, and actually makes it cost effective to produce in China and transport back to Argentina and the U.S. export market. What should the client do?

Interviewee: The client should consider looking for a joint venture Chinese partner with existing production facilities that will produce cost-effective chemical X for export back into Argentina given the time pressure. One key risk is that the joint venture partner may take unfair advantage of the client, given the client's unfamiliarity with China. So the client should aim to have a majority share of the joint venture.

If the client has more time, then it may want to consider building its own factory in China to have full ownership, but the key risk factor is the unfamiliarity in obtaining the necessary permits from the local Chinese government to build a factory focusing on a rather dangerous substance-chemical.

Firm: Do you want to quickly sum up what we have discussed, and assume that I am the client.

Interviewee: CEO, I would like to address your three concerns.

First, you do not face a threat to your domestic market because of the comparable production cost of chemical X between you and the Chinese producers. The transportation and tariff for the Chinese-produced chemical X will make it too costly to be competitive.

Second, you do not face an immediate threat to the U.S. export market because it costs more to transport Chinese-produced chemical X to the U.S. than from Argentina. However, you have to deepen your relationship with your U.S. customers, and ensure the Chinese produced chemical X will not be significantly less expensive than yours in the U.S. market moving forward. Therefore, you must always ensure your price is as competitive as the Chinese producers for your U.S. customers.

Third, you may not want to enter China now to produce chemical X because the Chinese domestic demand for chemical X has been more than fully met, and

Visit the Vault Consulting Career Channel at **www.vault.com/consulting** — with insider firm profiles, message boards, the Vault Consulting Job Board and more.

VAULT CAREER LIBRARY

41

there is no cost advantage for going to China to produce chemical X as compared to production in Argentina. That said, if it becomes much more cost effective to produce in China, then it is imperative to consider a joint venture partner in China to leverage on the more cost effective production process quickly.

Coffee Chain Market Entry Case

Sunshine Café is the fifth-largest coffee chain in the United States, with annual revenue of $500 million, and has no international presence. Sunshine Café operates coffee stores with a very similar format to Starbucks. It originated on the West Coast of the U.S., and has successfully served the Asian population in California very well. The CEO is now considering entering an Asian city to pursue revenue growth, with the longer-term plan of entering other Asian cities, but is unsure if it makes sense to do so.

Interviewee: I would like to clarify that the key question is whether Sunshine Café should enter one of the Asian cities, and, if so, how it should do so?

Firm: Yes, and make sure you can provide a preliminary plan for the CEO if she agrees that this market entry makes sense.

Interviewee: Before I jump into the case, I would like to take a step back and ask why the CEO wants to consider entering Asia.

Firm: That's a great question. Sunshine Café has experienced flat revenue over the past two to three years as the coffee chain market in the U.S. has increasingly matured. The CEO is looking for new growth revenue opportunities. She understands the need to invest for this expansion into Asia in the first couple of years.

Interviewee: Let me take a minute to lay out how I will approach this question. Will that be OK with you?

Firm: Sure.

(During the next 45 seconds, you lay out your framework clearly on a single sheet of paper.)

Interviewee: To answer the question, I would like to look into three broad areas. First, I want to understand the market size and growth for premium coffee consumption sold by coffee chains in key Asian cities. Second, I'd like to understand the competitive landscape, in terms of how competitive or fragmented each of the cities' market is. Third, I want to have more details on the ability of Sunshine Café to pursue international opportunities.

Firm: This approach seems reasonable. Which area do you want to focus on?

Interviewee: To better understand which Asian cities to choose, we should look at the potential market size and growth for coffee consumption sold by coffee chains. Do we have any information on which might be the most attractive markets?

Firm: What do you think?

Interviewee: Given that our coffee is going to be sold at a premium, I would like to focus on Asian cities where there are sufficient populations to purchase coffee at a premium. Also, given that we have no presence in Asia, it would be preferable to choose cities where foreign investors are welcome. Based on my understanding of Asia, Tokyo, Seoul, Hong Kong, Shanghai, Singapore and Sydney seem to be the larger, wealthier and friendlier cities for foreign investors.

Firm: That's a good first stab. In this case, do you mind doing a market sizing of the premium coffee chain drinking market in Hong Kong with a population of seven million?

Interviewee: I will use a bottom up approach, and show my thoughts and calculations on paper.

First, I want to determine how much regular and impulse customers will spend for coffee from coffee chains. Let's assume a regular drinker would buy from a coffee chain around twice a week, which is eight times a month, and around 96 times a year. Let's round that up to 100 cups/regular customer a year. An impulse drinker would maybe buy it twice a month, which is 24 cups a year, which I will round down to 20 cups/impulse customer a year. Assume a cup of coffee costs a weighted average of $2. Therefore, regular and impulse customers will spend $200/year and $40/year respectively.

Second, assume that individuals from ages 16 to 40 will buy coffee from a coffee chain, and the average life expectancy in Hong Kong is 70. Therefore, our potential customer base, based on age group, is $(40-16)/70$ = which is around 35 percent based on a linear age assumption. Thirty-five percent of seven million is around 2.4 million. Assume that 50 percent of this customer base will not buy coffee from coffee chains, so we are left with 1.2 million potential customers. Out of the 1.2 million potential customers, I assume around 25 percent are regular customers, and 75 percent are just impulse customers.

The 300,000 regular customers will therefore spend up to $60 million (300K*$200) a year and the 900,000 impulse customers will spend up to $36 million (900K*$40) a year. The Hong Kong market is $96 million or around $100 million.

Firm: Good. Do you think the Hong Kong market is attractive then?

Interviewee: Even if Sunshine Café can obtain 0.5 to 1 percent of the market, it will earn revenue of $500,000 to $1 million. How does that compare to a typical Starbucks store?

Firm: Great question. Starbucks reported revenue of $7.8 billion with 12,440 stores in 2006.

Interviewee: Assuming $8 billion and 12,500 stores, the average revenue per store is around $640,000. However, this number includes mainly U.S. stores, so the number may be lower for non-U.S. stores. Hong Kong appears to be a relatively attractive market to enter.

Firm: Good. A preliminary market sizing estimation shows that Hong Kong has a reasonable market size and growth rate as compared to other Asian cities. What do you think are the key drivers for the market growth for the cities?

Interviewee: There are two drivers. The first is the disposable income level, which will drive the percentage of the population able to purchase premium coffee and the frequency of purchase. The second is the uptake of "Western" influence. Buying expensive $2 coffee from coffee chains is a Western concept to many Asians, and more developed cities would have a greater number of customers who will purchase more coffee. Hong Kong has these two drivers to suggest a positive growth rate.

Firm: These are reasonable assumptions. Therefore, let's focus on entering the Hong Kong market for the remaining portion of this discussion. What about the competitive landscape?

Interviewee: We need to understand the saturation and concentration level of the Hong Kong coffee chain market. Being a developed city with significant Western influence, I assume that there are coffee chains in all attractive retail locations. If there are one or two major coffee chains that dominate the market, it may be difficult for Sunshine Café to penetrate Hong Kong unless we can better differentiate ourselves. The dominant players will have greater financial resources to bid up retail locations if they perceive that Sunshine Café will be a serious threat to them.

© 2008 Vault.com Inc.

Firm: The coffee chain market in Hong Kong is saturated but the market is relatively fragmented without any dominant players.

Interviewee: That's good to know. Can you share any insights into how the company has served the Asian population well in California that can actually help Sunshine Café successfully penetrate Hong Kong?

Firm: To attract the professionals who are its main, regular customers, Sunshine Café provides more electrical outlets for laptop users, universal chargers for mobile phones and a comprehensive delivery service to offices. To attract the local crowd, the café decorates and plays music targeted to the local crowds it serves. The individual café's décor is, therefore, slightly differentiated based on its location, but the quality of coffee is consistently high across all its stores.

Interviewee: Given this differentiation, Sunshine Café will likely be able to gain a foothold in the Hong Kong market. Going back to the third broad area of the framework, can I assume that since that they have been expanding throughout the U.S., their management team has recent experience in entering new markets?

Firm: Yes, the management team is confident about going into the international market.

Interviewee: I think I have sufficient information to provide some recommendations. May I have a minute to collect my thoughts?

Firm: Sure.

(Take a minute to think over your response.)

Interviewee: Sunshine Café should first enter the Hong Kong market by opening a flagship store, due to the attractiveness of the market. Sunshine Café must obtain a good retail location in a high traffic area and ensure high-quality coffee. The store must have the same features that made it attractive to Asian-Americans on the West Coast, but modified accordingly for the Hong Kong market. To be cost-effective, Sunshine Café must procure a comparable supplier of coffee beans at a competitive price relative to other coffee chains in Hong Kong.

The international management must be able to quickly learn the nuances of operating in Asia, and aim to open a second store in Hong Kong within six months, assuming the flagship store is projected to generate a reasonable return. After the first six months, the management should consider opening stores in Shanghai and Singapore, leveraging on what they've learned from operating the flagship store, and move on from there.

Visit the Vault Consulting Career Channel at **www.vault.com/consulting** — with insider firm profiles, message boards, the Vault Consulting Job Board and more.

V/\ULT CAREER LIBRARY   **45**

The key risk factor in opening stores in Asia is the need to learn how to deal with the different governments, and choosing to open stores initially in foreign investor-friendly cities such as Hong Kong, Singapore and Shanghai will help to alleviate the risk.

Consumer Products Growth Strategy Case

Case facts initially offered by the interviewer

• The client is a large consumer products company.
• The client desires to substantially increase the size of its operations.
• The client also wants to introduce the Internet as a distribution channel.
• The client's goal is to double total sales and profits in less than three to five years.

Questions to be answered by candidate

• What steps would you undertake?
• What issues would you consider?

Suggested solutions

The candidate has two parts to address in this case. One is whether to introduce the Internet as a distribution channel and the other is to increase sales and profitability.

Before suggesting any action, the candidate must attempt to understand the existing operations of the company and its distribution networks. Some questions can also aid the candidate to get a better sense for the company's current customers, as well as potential customers, to see if the Internet is a viable delivery mechanism for the company.

The following are questions and answers that would be provided in an interview scenario.

Interviewee: What is the current "Value Chain" of the client?

Firm: The client is a retailer and wholesaler for white good appliances. The retail segment is becoming more attractive in recent times, especially the last one to two years.

Interviewee: Is the Internet, as a distribution channel, already operational in the client's market segment? In retail or wholesale (i.e., B2B or B2C)?

Firm: The Internet is gaining popularity in the retail segment only.

Interviewee: What is the current market size of the retail market in which the client is operating?

Firm: Current market size: $2 billion, client's share: 15 percent.

Interviewee: How is the market segmented within the client's operations?

Firm: Client has three market segments that operate as profit centers. The market segments are refrigerators, washing machines and dishwashers. The client's revenue is roughly evenly divided among all three market segments.

Interviewee: What is the competitive nature of the industry? What would the effect be on sales and profits if we simply reduced prices or margins?

Firm: Fluctuation in prices does not affect competition in a major way, though it does have an impact on the bottom line if any of the major players bring the prices down considerably. The client's margins are found to be consistent with industry norms.

Interviewee: What is the current distribution network undertaken by the client?

Firm: The client has six retail shops and the wholesale market is catered to directly from the warehouse.

Interviewee: How is the competition adapting to Internet technology in the retail market?

Firm: In the retail market, two competitors have emerged in the Internet shopping business, and are rapidly gaining market share. One of the companies that have already entered this new marketplace is the client's primary competitor in the traditional market. The second is a pure online player who entered the market recently in the target region with Internet shopping and delivery services. The Internet is popular only in the wholesale segment.

Interviewee: Who are the client's major competitors in this market?

Firm: Current competition includes four leading players and numerous other smaller players. Three of them operate just like the client, both in retail and wholesale market.

Interviewee: Can you tell me the market share of these players?

Firm: The new online player has captured 8 percent of the market in the last year. The other three have approximately 20 percent market share.

Interviewee: Can you tell me a little about the client's customers in the existing retail market to see if the Internet is a viable delivery mechanism for the company?

Firm: The client serves primarily upper middle-class customers.

Interviewee: That's important to know. I would guess that prospective users of an Internet-based system are upper middle class. Can you confirm this and elaborate on the growth prospects for this market?

Firm: Your guess is correct. Users of the Internet system are typically upper middle class. As far as the market is concerned, online shopping among Internet users is growing rapidly and the percentage of homes with Internet access is also growing.

Interviewee: I'd like to now focus on our client. Clearly not all companies are prepared to put their operations on the Internet. The central issues I'd like to better understand are the company's core competencies—does it have the requisite skills to address the Internet user? Do you have any information on the company's distribution capabilities? Specifically, is it able to address the Internet market?

Firm: The client's current distribution facilities are not adequate for the delivery system.

Interviewee: How about the company's employees? Are they sufficiently trained to handle delivery tasks associated with the Internet?

Firm: The current employees cannot perform these tasks without more training.

Possible steps/analysis regarding the Internet as a distribution network

A quick three Cs Analysis may be used (company, customer, competition) from the gathered information and the following can be inferred.

• Given the market attractiveness for Internet orders, the client would be remiss to pass up this opportunity.

• Its customers are high-potential Internet users.

• The competition has already shown a willingness to invest in the market, and the competitor with no stores in the region (i.e., totally reliant on Internet sales) is growing the fastest.

© 2008 Vault.com Inc.

- That said, the company must be willing to invest in this market to succeed.

  - First, it must improve its distribution capabilities.

  - Further analysis must be done as to whether it should improve its current operations or develop a stand-alone capability exclusively devoted to the Internet market.

  - Next, it must develop an inventory management system so that it can effectively track what it orders from suppliers, what customers are ordering and where the product is delivered (Internet vs. traditional).

  - Finally, it must spend enough money to cross-train its employees so that tasks associated with Internet delivery can be effectively performed.

Regarding the client's goal to double sales and profits in the next three years, the following probing can be done

Interviewee: Has the client already considered any plans for market expansion?

Firm: The client is considering acquiring a small retail firm in the retail market.

Interviewee: What potential is there for expansion by acquisition?

Firm: As mentioned earlier, that are quite a few small players in this market and they control about 20 percent of the market share.

Interviewee: Has the client researched any target companies in the wholesale market?

Firm: No.

Interviewee: Any insights on the competitive scenario of the wholesale market?

Firm: The client is a market leader in that segment, controlling 40 percent of the market share.

Interviewee: Is the client looking into expanding its operations in that segment?

Firm: No.

Interviewee: Do the target company and the client compete in the same geographical areas?

Firm: The target firm has three stores and these stores cater to the sectors not in the client's area of operation.

Visit the Vault Consulting Career Channel at www.vault.com/consulting — with insider firm profiles, message boards, the Vault Consulting Job Board and more.

VAULT CAREER LIBRARY   49

Interviewee: How strong is the target firm's presence in the local market?

Firm: Being a smaller firm, it has strong contacts with many local customers, and is often the preferred supplier due to its customer responsiveness.

Interviewee: Does the potential target firm have any technological capability for Internet sales?

Firm: No research has been done on that.

Interviewee: Does the company have the financial capability?

Firm: The client has the financial capability to finance the acquisition internally.

Possible analysis for market expansion

A business can increase profits in three ways:

1. Increasing sales
2. Increasing prices
3. Decreasing costs

However, given that the company's margins are found to be consistent with industry norms, it would seem unlikely that either increasing prices or cutting costs represents a feasible method by which to double sales and profits, particularly if the company is operating in a moderately competitive environment. This leaves only sales increases, which could be achieved by:

• Selling more of the current products to current customers
• Selling new products to current customers
• Selling current products to new customers
• Selling new products to new customers

The suitability of these options will again depend on the particular environment. In this case, it turned out that only selling new products to new customers via some form of diversification could help achieve the company goals.

The client should then consider the potential for increasing sales by means of diversification through acquisition. Since there is synergy between the target firm and the client's operations, and the acquisition will increase the market reach of the client.

Possible recommendations

• To sell new products to new customers by means of acquiring the target firm.

• Be active in the retail market using both brick and mortar and Internet channels of distribution.

 © 2008 Vault.com Inc.

- Eliminate cannibalization by focusing on distinct products for each channel.

- Continue operations in the wholesale market, in which the client has a strong presence.

Key takeaways

This case can prove to be lengthy and very involved given the two components that are expected to be solved by the candidate. It is not expected that a candidate would cover all of the above topics, but rather work through selected topics in a logical fashion. It is important that the candidate pursue a solution that is holistic, and understand the complete nature of the Internet as a viable distribution channel. The above suggested recommendations for improving growth prospects and pursuing the Internet channel are just a few among many. The candidate may come up with his or her own ideas.

Credit Card Company Revenue Growth Case

A leading credit card company has seen its revenue growth decline in recent years. It used to have over 10 percent annual growth, and in recent years it's been less. For example, the client had a revenue of $17 billion two years ago and $18 billion this past year. It has hired us to help develop ideas to jumpstart its revenue growth to get it back to 10 percent in the next couple years.

Additional information provided during questioning

- The client is a large financial services provider, but the majority of its revenue comes from its credit card business. Its other businesses include an asset management firm, a private wealth management advisory firm and a small business loan company.

- The business model for the credit card business is as follows: The company makes money from two sources: 1) revenue from interest payments from cardholders who carry a balance from month to month, and 2) revenue from merchants who accept the card. This credit card company takes 3 to 5 percent of all purchases made with the card from merchants and a flat fee of $30/month from merchants for the telecom charges for transactions, rental of the swipe machine and basic servicing of the merchants' accounts.

- Credit cards have been around since the 1950s, but the industry really took off in the U.S. in the 1980s and has continued to expand globally. This case will

Visit the Vault Consulting Career Channel at **www.vault.com/consulting** — with insider firm profiles, message boards, the Vault Consulting Job Board and more.

VAULT CAREER LIBRARY

51

focus on the U.S. market only, as internationally, the client's revenue is still growing quickly from year to year.

This case begins with some interviewer questions that test the interviewee's basic business sense or instincts, then moves into the more typical structure of a case interview. This beginning part may throw an interviewee off, but it's a good example of how an interviewer might test to see if a candidate has a good general business sense and comfort talking about business issues.

After the initial questioning, this really turns into a marketing case about a new product introduction. This case is best solved using the marketing framework of the 4Ps. There are numbers thrown into the case mainly to test quantitative ability (and there are a few numbers tests sprinkled throughout), but one of the main pieces of quantitative analysis does drive the final "answer" to the case.

It's important that the interviewee understand the credit card company business model and that there are two sources of revenue for the company (cardholders and merchants). If the interviewee does not probe this, the interviewer will make sure that they understand the business model.

Breakdown of solution

Firm: So, first, do you have any questions?

Interviewee: Sure. I want to just be certain that I understand the problem. The client is a large credit card company. It has seen its revenue growth decline in recent years, and it's looking for a few good ideas to help jumpstart it in the next two years. Is that correct?

Firm: Yes, that's right.

Interviewee: Also, I'm not that familiar with the credit card business, but my understanding is that those firms make their money both from the interest paid by people who have credit cards and from merchants, as some sort of percentage of the charges.

Firm: Yes, that's right. Merchants also pay a monthly fee for transaction equipment, operations and servicing—so, it's kind of a wash for the credit card companies. But technically, it is revenue. So, you seem to know a good amount about the credit card business. Let's start with a couple of quick questions about the industry just to get a sense of the big picture.

Interviewee: Okay.

© 2008 Vault.com Inc.

(Here's where the interviewer wants to test the interviewee's general business sense/instincts. The interviewer is not looking for an exact answer—just a directionally-correct sense.)

Firm: On the following spectrum of young and growing to mature and slow, where would you put the credit card industry in the U.S.?

Credit Card Industry in U.S.

Young, fast-growing industry   Mature, slow-growing industry

(The interviewee should mark on the spectrum, or answer directionally.)

Interviewee: Probably more on the slow and mature side, especially since I know this client is seeing revenue growth problems.

Firm: That's right. On the spectrum of highly differentiated and branded to commoditized and interchangeable, where would you put credit cards as a product?

Credit Card Industry in US

Undifferentiated, commodity product   HIghly differentiated, branded product

---

(The interviewee should mark on spectrum, or answer directionally.)

Interviewee: While I do see a fair amount of credit card advertising, I basically think of them as being the same—with the interest rate as the main differentiator for me. So, I'll say that they're more of a price-based commodity.

Firm: That's right. Sure, credit card companies in the U.S. have tried to brand themselves, but my sense is that this branding has less effect than with many other types of products. Okay, well, now that we have a good sense of the industry, let's go back to the original question. The client's revenue growth has slowed. From what you know, what's been their recent year-over-year growth in revenue?

Visit the Vault Consulting Career Channel at **www.vault.com/consulting** — with insider firm profiles, message boards, the Vault Consulting Job Board and more.

VAULT CAREER LIBRARY   **53**

Interviewee: Well, you mentioned that two years ago, the company's revenue was $17 billion, and the next year, it was $18 billion. That's a growth of $1 billion, which is about a 6 percent growth.

(Growth rate = ($18-17)/17 billion = 1/17 = .058, which can be rounded to 6 percent)

Firm: Yes, that's right. And what is it aiming for?

Interviewee: You mentioned that they were used to over 10 percent annual growth in revenue. So it used to almost double that.

Firm: That's right. From last year, when annual revenue was $18 billion, what type of revenue do you think it's aiming for this year?

($18 billion X 10 percent = 1.8 billion; $18 billion + 1.8 = $19.8 billion, which is approximately $20 billion)

Interviewee: Well, if it wants at least 10 percent annual revenue growth, then it would probably like to see about $20 billion in revenue, which means around $2 billion in new revenue in the year.

Firm: That's about right—$2 billion in a year. So, let's go back to the original question now that we know what the numbers goal is for this revenue growth. How would you structure how to look at jumpstarting that revenue growth?

Interviewee: Can I take a few minutes to collect my thoughts?

Firm: Of course.

(After a couple minutes ...)

Interviewee: Since this case is about growing revenue, I would divide my analysis into four primary buckets that effect revenue: 1) our products, 2) our price, 3) our promotional and marketing activities, and 4) our distribution/geographic reach/placement of our products.

(Any sort of 4Ps derivation would work effectively here. The interviewee may want to disguise the Ps, or customize them to the credit card industry, but it's not necessary. Getting the correct structure is the hardest part.)

Firm: That's a great way to look at it. Do you have any thoughts on where you might want to start, or which might be the most fruitful buckets for ideas to grow revenue?

Interviewee: Well, if I step back and think about our earlier discussion of the credit card industry, we said that it was a more mature industry and credit cards are more of a commodity/less branded product. So, that makes me think that

© 2008 Vault.com Inc.

price is hard to move upwards for a commodity product, and it also makes me think that changing our products' marketing or promotional activities will have less of an impact on revenue growth. So, that leaves the product and the placement of that product as the two buckets to explore. Are there geographic opportunities outside the U.S. that we should explore?

Firm: First off, great job—price and promotion are definitely not the biggest triggers for revenue for credit cards. Second, there are geographic opportunities outside the U.S. that the client is exploring—and your hunch is right about expanding international placement of the client's product. But for now, the client wants us to focus on jumpstarting revenue in the U.S.

That leaves looking at the product, and that's actually where the case took us. One of the things that we looked at for the client was launching a new product for the company in the U.S.—a gift card product aimed at consumers. We found that there had been real growth in gift cards in the retail industry—in fact, top U.S. retailers' gift cards given at Christmas accounted for $10 billion last year, and we thought that this sort of product lent itself perfectly to the client's capabilities, current infrastructure, etc. Do you know what I mean by a gift card?

Interviewee: I think so. I'm assuming it's like a fixed-value credit card, with an amount stored on it, that a cardholder could purchase to give to someone else, but that it would basically function much like a credit card.

Firm: Exactly—and be used anywhere that someone could use a credit card. Now, given our original mandate for the case from the client, how would you evaluate whether or not this is a good idea?

Interviewee: Well, if I look back in my notes, my understanding is that we need to bring the client three ideas to help it bring back its revenue growth to 10 percent annually that it could implement in the next one to two years. It sounds like—because the infrastructure for these cards is the same as that for credit cards—that this gift card idea could be implemented in that one- to two-year time frame. Is that correct?

Firm: Yes, it is. Now, just to give you a sense of how the business model would work, the client would continue to see two revenue streams from the product: one from the merchant in terms of 3 percent of the purchase and one from the consumer purchasing the card, let's say a 2 percent service charge. So, let's assume that each idea that we bring to the client needs to be at least a $50 million idea in the first year that requires no significant infrastructure investment. Do you think this could be one?

Visit the Vault Consulting Career Channel at **www.vault.com/consulting** — with insider firm profiles, message boards, the Vault Consulting Job Board and more.

VAULT CAREER LIBRARY

55

Interviewee: Well, you mentioned that currently, top U.S. retailers sell $10 billion annually around the holidays in gift cards. Let's say that because we could cut across ALL retailers in the U.S., we could get a 10 percent market share of the gift card market within one to two years. That's owning $1 billion of the gift cards sold in the U.S.—if we just look at the holidays.

Firm: Yeah, let's just look at the holidays for now—they make up the majority of gift card purchases anyway.

Interviewee: Okay, so, we sell $1 billion gift cards, but our revenue from that amount is the 3 percent of that paid by merchants and the 2 percent of that paid by card purchasers. That means that our revenue from a new gift card product would be about $50 million, which is just the size of the type of idea that we're looking for.

Firm: That's right. So, how might you summarize this case?

Interviewee: Well, if I look back at the original question of the case, this company needs several ideas to jumpstart its revenue growth in the U.S. market, and it's hoping to see ideas that will add $1 billion in sales in the next couple years. Since the credit card industry is fairly mature in the U.S. and credit cards are more of a commodity product, the company should focus on new product introductions that require little or no investment in additional infrastructure—like gift cards—to achieve that renewed growth.

Firm: That's great.

EU Customs Brokers Case

Your client operates a network of customs brokers in the U.S. and has offices in one or two major cities of most states. The company now wants to expand its business into the EU countries using a similar business model, except instead of different states, it would carry out customs brokerage for goods traded between different EU countries. It has decided it needs to come into the market in a big way and plan to eventually have at least one office in each country. But it is not sure how to choose staffing allocations for different offices or even where it needs to have offices initially.

It has asked you to help it think through this problem. It does not need you to identify precisely how many brokers are needed in each country or which countries to target first. Rather, it wants you to help it develop a framework for planning office locations and develop some kind of scale for where the smallest to largest offices need to be. How would you help it work through this?

© 2008 Vault.com Inc.

(This is an industry you are very likely to be completely unfamiliar with. Do not hesitate to ask a few questions to gain some basic information about it and the client's work. Use the information to begin thinking about how you want to structure your analysis.)

Interviewee: Could you please tell me about the customs brokerage industry? I have a few thoughts, but being unfamiliar with it, I would not want to start structuring my analysis based on some assumptions.

Firm: Sure. The basic function of customs brokers is to work with their clients, businesses or individuals, on one hand, and with the countries' or states' customs authorities on the other. In the U.S., so far they have been assisting their business or individual clients import goods into the U.S. through their expertise in legal requirements, taxes and duties and so on. Customs officials usually prefer to work with them as well because they can speak a common language, which expedites their work. Our client works only with shipments having goods that are individually classified under $100,000 in value. In the European expansion, it plans to also deal with exports and not just imports.

Interviewee: How were the offices set up in the U.S. geographically? What was the thinking behind choosing locations, staff allocations and so on?

Firm: Well, in the U.S. things have happened quite haphazardly rather than through any great strategic plan. The client established offices in one or two major cities initially and gradually just added cities where it found work, thereby growing one city at a time. Offices were scaled up and down, sometimes quite rapidly, based on demand and this has often led to losses from lost business, downsizing and so on. It is exactly this kind of unplanned growth that the client wants to avoid this time by thinking through where the offices need to be, and which ones can be small or larger.

(You now have some background information and should think about how to structure the case moving forward. You can always ask the interviewer to give you a minute or two. Most will prefer you take the time to do this, rather than ask a series of questions that seem like shots in the dark.)

Interviewee: I'd like to structure my analysis as follows. I first need to understand what drives the decision to set up an office in a particular place, and then the factors that contribute to its staffing requirements. I'd like to use successful offices in particular U.S. locations as examples, and see if there are any lessons to be learned from them. Once I understand these drivers, I would like to try to apply them to the EU countries to see if we can prioritize where our client should set up country offices and which locations might be larger than others.

Visit the Vault Consulting Career Channel at www.vault.com/consulting — with insider firm profiles, message boards, the Vault Consulting Job Board and more.

VAULT CAREER LIBRARY

57

Firm: I think that's OK. For the sake of simplicity assume that if you set up an office in a country, it will be in the capital only. In other words, you do not need to think about multiple cities in a single country.

Interviewee: OK. I'll start with looking at why a particular location may be selected for an office. Based on what you've told me, the main function of a broker is to assist with the legal and other aspects of goods that are being imported or exported. My assumption would be that this kind of work will mainly occur where the actual trade is taking place, and in the long run the office would need to be located at those centers of trade or very close to them, assuming that other costs such as commercial space, human resources, etc., are not large enough to offset the importance of being next to the location of trade.

Firm: Yes, that seems reasonable.

Interviewee: One driver that would determine the amount of resources required is the amount of trade that takes place. Therefore, I would further assume that places having greater trade—interstate in the U.S. or international in Europe—are candidates for larger offices.

Firm: Yes, that is a slightly simplified description, but a fair assumption to move forward with.

(As you go along, it is sometimes helpful to summarize your information and assumptions. This will not only help the interviewer have a clearer picture of how you are progressing, but also allows you to periodically take stock of your work to see if you have made any errors or overlooked anything.)

Interviewee: Just to review the analysis so far, it seems that the main driver for an office location is to be near a trade center. Additionally, higher volumes of trade generally imply the need for larger size offices assuming that commercial space and other operating costs are not exceptionally high. Are there any other critical factors that we can ascertain from studying the successful U.S. offices?

Firm: No, I think those are the biggest drivers.

Interviewee: I'd like to apply these to locations in Europe. Our client deals in shipments of goods valued less than $100,000. Does the client have any data on shipping volumes for different locations in Europe?

Firm: No, there is no such data currently available. How would you propose the company could get this kind of data?

Interviewee: There may be market data already available either from previous market research or from government sources. If there isn't, the company may

 © 2008 Vault.com Inc.

need to conduct such market research or hire an appropriate firm to do it for them.

Firm: No, there is no such data available. You are correct, the client may eventually need to hire a firm to collect such data at some point. However, that would be expensive and would probably take quite some time. Can you suggest something that the client could do as a first estimate? This would help it with some initial planning, and can even help it decide if it needs more precise data.

(At this point you have an opportunity to show some creativity. Consultants often have to look for data relevant to a poorly defined situation and use it to develop estimates. They will use these estimates in the absence of or until better data can be found, and it is a skill you can benefit from displaying in your interview. Try to step back and think about what kind of data may be similar to what you are looking for. In this case, you are dealing with a subsection of trade that comprises goods valued under a specific amount. You could assume that trends in the trade of such goods are similar to trends in general trade between countries. You may not be completely correct—but when making estimates, your assumptions need to be reasonable rather than completely accurate. Be sure to state the assumptions you are making when you use them.)

Interviewee: An assumption I would make here is that trends in the kind of trade our client deals with mirror trends in overall trade of countries. For example, if the total trade throughout France is double that of Spain, then the trade in goods valued under $100,000 in France is also double that of Spain. I realize this may not be true for all countries, but it may be sufficient for a first analysis. We should be able to get the information for overall country trade volumes from both government and other sources such as the WTO.

Firm: OK, so how would you proceed with this assumption?

Interviewee: Do we have information on what countries are involved in the greatest amount of trading?

Firm: Let's assume France, Germany, Spain, Belgium and Ireland are the countries with the top-five volumes of trade.

Interviewee: Based on my assumption, these would also be the countries with the highest volume of trade in goods valued under $100,000. Given your earlier simplification, their capital cities would potentially be the first five locations to establish offices. These five cities I would rank in terms of largest to smallest in the same order as their trade volume. Beyond these five, the remaining EU countries would also be ranked per their trade volume.

Visit the Vault Consulting Career Channel at www.vault.com/consulting — with insider firm profiles, message boards, the Vault Consulting Job Board and more.

VAULT CAREER LIBRARY

59

Firm: Based on your assumptions so far, that is a reasonable ranking to produce. These assumptions are based on the U.S. business structure. Do you see any anything different about Europe that may require changes to how the business operates and plans its office structure?

Interviewee: The one big difference between the U.S. and European operations will be that in the U.S. the company brokers probably only need to be familiar with U.S. law, since they're dealing with imports only. When moving to Europe and dealing with both imports and exports, there might be a need for specialized brokers who are aware of the requirements of different countries.

Firm: Correct, that will be a big difference. How do you think the company could estimate the placing of such specialist brokers? For example how would the company estimate if it needs more brokers specializing in German trade law than Spanish trade law, in its French office?

(You are still dealing with factors that affect a trading center. There are two main variables, the quantity of trade and where the trade is coming from or going to—the "tradelane." You have worked your way through the first part and should now think about the second one.)

Interviewee: The requirement for specialized broker knowledge depends on the countries trading with one another. For example, if France trades significantly more often with Germany than with Spain, then by my earlier assumption, it is trading more with Germany than with Spain for goods valued under $100,000. In this case it would need to have more brokers trained in German law than in Spanish law in the French office.

Firm: Could you make this kind of assessment for the different countries?

Interviewee: Continuing with the earlier assumption, I would again use the trade between different countries as a proxy. Governments will be publishing details of their trade volumes with different countries as would nongovernmental organizations such as the WTO. We could construct a table of all the EU countries and fill in the value of the trade between each of them. This tabulation will highlight those tradelanes with the maximum activity.

(If you have a paper and pen, it may be helpful to your interviewer if you quickly sketch out the table as you describe it, so as to eliminate any confusion he/she may have.)

Firm: Is there any further refinement you can make to the proxy?

Interviewee: So far, we have looked at overall trade values. We could potentially split this up into import and export volumes between countries. I think

© 2008 Vault.com Inc.

this information should also be available from the same sources, that is, government released data or organizations such as the WTO.

Firm: I think that's reasonable. Thank you.

Case analysis

This case is about providing your client with some guidelines for how to set up its new organizational structure. At the very start you were told that the interviewer is not looking for precise numbers. This implies that he or she wants to explore this case on a conceptual level to see if you can develop a framework that the client could then use with the actual numbers. You also had the benefit of the U.S. example and so were not starting from scratch. However, it is important to evaluate what had worked in the U.S. and what had not, and also to think about what might be different in the EU.

When developing recommendations on a conceptual/framework level, as you go along you should do periodic reality checks with yourself on what you are suggesting. It is possible that the interviewer could decide to test you on your recommendations by providing real data and asking you to use it in your framework. If you have been doing some reality checks on your work, you have a better chance of not deriving unexpected results. If you do arrive at an unexpected result, do not panic. Acknowledge that the result seems off, and look systematically for possible flaws in your assumptions and framework, or for any calculation or mathematical errors you may have made.

Eyewear Chain Case

Eye Inc., an eyewear chain, has been struggling with declining per store revenue and profit recently as it underwent expansion in the past 10 years. The founder wants us to determine the reason for the decline, and how she should address it. The successful eyewear firm believes that it is providing a valuable service to its regular customers, and not just selling products, which are the lens and frames. Most successful eyewear firms aim to establish and build strong relationships with their customers.

Firm: Your team has spent some time analyzing the revenue and profitability of the same store sales. What can you infer from this slide?

Visit the Vault Consulting Career Channel at www.vault.com/consulting — with insider firm profiles, message boards, the Vault Consulting Job Board and more.

VAULT CAREER LIBRARY

61

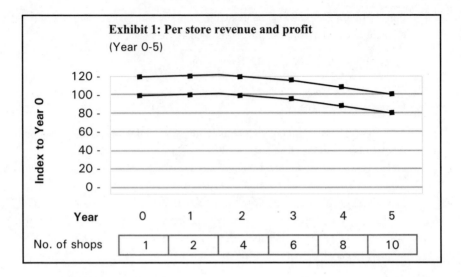

Exhibit 1: Per store revenue and profit
(Year 0-5)

Year	0	1	2	3	4	5
No. of shops	1	2	4	6	8	10

Interviewee: Revenue and profit appears to be declining at the same rate, which means that cost is not likely to be an issue. Therefore, we should definitely look into what is driving the declining revenue, which has resulted in the declining profit. Given that revenue constitutes volume of eyewear sold multiplied by the price of eyewear, we need to determine whether price or volume is driving the decline in revenue.

Firm: That sounds like a good plan moving forward. How would you like to proceed?

Interviewee: Let's focus on the price. Do we have any data to show that the average price of eyewear has declined?

Firm: Before I answer the question, I would like to know what you think are the key drivers for the price of eyewear.

Interviewee: In order to determine what may be driving price down, it is important to analyze the client's expansion plan. Eye Inc. may have expanded into a market saturated with existing eyewear retailers, and therefore the limited market may have encouraged the price competition. Another reason may be that Eye Inc. is trying to attract new customers by offering a significant price cut in their new stores through a penetration pricing strategy, and finds it challenging to increase the price while retaining the same volume of customers.

Firm: Both are good reasons why price may be a driver for the revenue decline. However, Eye Inc. is acutely aware of the damaging implication of price wars, and therefore has not been engaging in these as it opens new stores. It

© 2008 Vault.com Inc.

has also chosen its locations carefully, taking into account existing competition, threshold population and access to the stores.

Interviewee: OK, let's explore the volume side then. If price has remained relatively constant, then the volume of eyewear purchased must have dropped. Do we have any data to show how the volume of eyewear purchased has declined over time?

Firm: What specific data do you think will be helpful in determining the drivers for the decline of volume?

Interviewee: The decline in volume may be due to unfavorable location of the retail shop or the decrease in customer satisfaction. However, we have assessed that the locations were selected carefully, so any data focusing on customer satisfaction will be helpful.

Firm: Eye Inc. actually does segment its customers between regular and non-regular customers. It defines its regular customers as those who have purchased more than one eyewear product within a year. Here's the data made available to us. What can you infer from it?

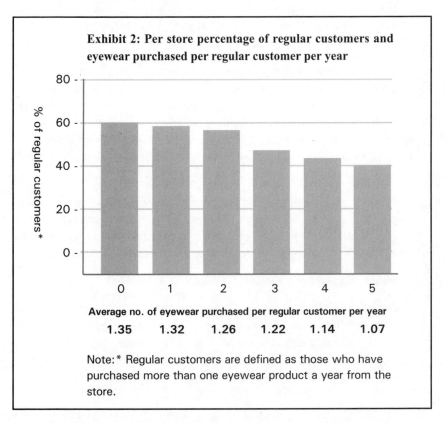

Exhibit 2: Per store percentage of regular customers and eyewear purchased per regular customer per year

% of regular customers *

Average no. of eyewear purchased per regular customer per year
1.35   1.32   1.26   1.22   1.14   1.07

Note: * Regular customers are defined as those who have purchased more than one eyewear product a year from the store.

Visit the Vault Consulting Career Channel at www.vault.com/consulting — with insider firm profiles, message boards, the Vault Consulting Job Board and more.

VAULT CAREER LIBRARY   63

Interviewee: The number of regular customers has actually declined over time, and even the client's regular customers are buying fewer pieces of eyewear. Given that cost has not changed based on the first slide, my hypothesis is that Eye Inc. has been reducing services to all of its customers to keep cost constant in the midst of rapid expansion, which resulted in the decline of regular customers.

Firm: Before we discuss why that will specifically drive the decline of regular customers, can you calculate the percentage drop in regular eyewear contribution to Eye Inc. in Year 0 as compared to Year 5?

Interviewee: A non-regular customer only purchases one eyewear product in one year. Therefore, the index for Year 1 is 1.40*60 percent +1*40 percent = 1.24. The index for Year 5 is 1.07*40 percent +1*60 percent = 1.03. The percentage drop is (1.24 - 1.03) / 1.24 = 17 percent drop. Given that the revenue has declined from an index of 100 to 80, a 20 percent drop from Year 0 to Year 5, the declines in regular customers and purchases of eyewear products by regular customers are the key drivers.

Firm: Let's go back to discussing—what do you think caused these declines?

Interviewee: Regular customers are important contributors to the revenue and profitability of an eyewear business. Therefore, Eye Inc. most likely has reduced the services provided to regular customers to keep costs down.

Customers tend to return to the shop to have their frames fixed or lenses replaced due to minor scratches, and the more successful eyewear firms may only charge a minimal sum or waive the charges altogether to strengthen customer relationships. In addition, goodwill is generated at this specific occasion when regular customers are in the stores and have their needs met with minimal cost and fuss, and these regular customers may be persuaded to purchase other eyewear products such as an extra frame or sunglasses.

However, if customers felt that they were not provided the extra service support and were charged more than a token sum for these repairs, it is unlikely they will buy a new eyewear product or even return to the store. This explains the decline in average number of eyewear products for the regular customers.

Firm: What will your recommendation to the founder be?

Interviewee: In order for the Eye Inc. to arrest the decline of revenue and profit, the founder needs to evaluate the decision to manage costs by cutting down services rendered to the stores' regular customers. Regular customers significantly contribute to the revenue of each store, especially with repeat purchases. It is therefore critical to ensure that the percentage of regular customers

© 2008 Vault.com Inc.

does not dip by continuing to provide after-care services, and creating opportunities for the regular customers to purchase more eyewear products.

However, it is important to ensure that the cost of providing these after-care services does not negate the benefit from increasing purchases by more regular customers. At the least, it is still important to prioritize these after-care services to those who have been regular customers.

Health Care CPG Consumer Loyalty Program Case

A large CPG (consumer packaged goods) company specializing in health care products is a client of our consulting firm. The CEO was discussing several business issues on his mind with one of our consulting firm's senior partners, and one of the topics that came up was consumer loyalty programs. The CEO would love to do a loyalty program for the company's target consumers, but has asked us whether this is a good idea. How would you structure that inquiry?

Additional information provided during questioning

• The client is a large health care-related products manufacturer and distributor. While about 25 percent of business is composed of products for doctors and other health care professionals, the majority of its products are targeted towards consumers (think soaps and shampoos, cotton swabs, diapers, etc.). The case will focus on that part of its business.

• The client's target consumer for its CPG business tends to be mothers, as those are the consumers doing the purchasing of most household items.

• This client is one of the firm's largest in the U.S. As such, the firm has a fairly close relationship with the CEO, and the CEO often uses the firm as his own "strategic planning group." He runs his ideas through the firm to see if there's a viable business case before making decisions and executing them.

• Customer loyalty programs have a long history. Some of the most well-known loyalty programs include frequent flyer miles, where loyal customers accumulate miles for paid-for travel, and which can be traded in for upgrades, free travel or other gifts. These "frequent user" programs have been mimicked by banks, credit card companies, hotel chains and rental car companies. However, loyalty programs have also existed in the CPG realm. For decades, consumers have been induced to repeatedly buy brands due to gifts and offers, which hinge upon collecting the UPC labels of packaged goods.

Visit the Vault Consulting Career Channel at www.vault.com/consulting — with insider firm profiles, message boards, the Vault Consulting Job Board and more.

VAULT CAREER LIBRARY   65

Suggested high-level overview of solution

There are two concepts that should really be used to structure and solve the case. The first is cost-benefit analysis, and the second is opportunity cost. As long as an interviewee hits on those two concepts, he or she should be able to find a solution to the case.

There's a lot of background information here, and up-front hints about the delicacy and importance of this client relationship. A successful interviewee will likely spend a good bit of time probing the context of the client relationship and the nature of the client's idea before even attempting to solve the case.

Breakdown of solution (including quantitative analyses and qualitative evaluations)

Interviewee: I'd like to make sure that I understand the case. So, our client is a health care CPG company. Does that mean that it sells products like cold medicine?

Firm: You're on the right track. It is a health care CPG, and it does sell a couple of over-the-counter illness remedies like cold medicine and aspirin. But actually, its main product lines are more like cotton swabs, soaps and diapers. Some of its products are also geared more towards doctors and nurses, but our client wants us to focus on consumer loyalty programs, and the consumer side of its business.

Interviewee: Great, that gives me a better understanding of the type of company we're talking about. Now, I'd like to get a better sense of the firm's relationship with this client. You mentioned that this client is one of the largest for the firm, and that the CEO has a pretty close relationship to at least one of the senior partners here. It sounds like the firm has a pretty good relationship with this client, and the CEO in particular.

Firm: Yes, that's correct. The CEO often uses our firm as his own sort of "strategic planning group." He runs his ideas through us to develop the business case before he presents it internally to his company for execution. He's pretty excited about this loyalty program idea—he loves his frequent flyer memberships and wants to see if he can do something like that for his company's consumers.

Interviewee: In terms of the consumers, who exactly is the company's target audience?

Firm: That's a great question. The client's target consumer for its CPG business tends to be mothers, as those do the purchasing for most household items. Does that answer all of your questions?

Interviewee: Just one more: In terms of consumer loyalty programs, what exactly is in the realm of possibilities? I mean, I know that the CEO is thinking about his frequent flyer membership card, but how does that translate to health care packaged goods exactly?

Firm: That's another great question. We actually ended up doing a lot of research into a variety of consumer loyalty programs. Customer loyalty programs have a long history. Some of the most well-known loyalty programs are the airline frequent flyer miles, where loyal customers accumulate miles for paid-for travel that can then be traded in for upgrades, free travel or other gifts. These "frequent user" programs have been mimicked by banks, credit card companies, hotel chains and rental car companies. However, loyalty programs have also existed in the CPG area. For decades, consumers have been induced to repeatedly buy brands in order to get gifts and offers that are based on the collection of a certain number of UPC labels on packaged goods. Does that give you a better sense of what's out there?

Interviewee: Yes. Can I have a few moments to compose my thoughts?

Firm: Of course.

(A couple of minutes later ...)

Interviewee: So, the question that the client has put forth is to decide whether a consumer loyalty program is a good idea. In order to evaluate this, we would need to do some sort of a cost-benefit analysis to see how much extra revenue in sales we might get from the program versus what it costs to run it.

Firm: That's right. And that's exactly what we did. Now, I'd like to show you some benchmarking data that we did on different pilot consumer loyalty programs out there—none that our client is specifically running—but this research aided us in helping the client think about starting a new program.

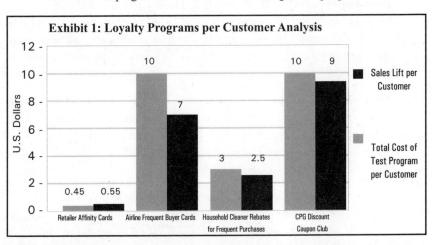

Exhibit 1: Loyalty Programs per Customer Analysis

Visit the Vault Consulting Career Channel at **www.vault.com/consulting** — with insider firm profiles, message boards, the Vault Consulting Job Board and more.

VAULT CAREER LIBRARY

67

So, what does this data tell you?

Interviewee: Let me make sure that I'm reading this correctly. Each of these sets of bars represents the per customer sales lift and the costs of pilot consumer loyalty programs of other companies?

Firm: Yes. That's right. Which program is the best?

(Now, the interviewee needs to do some quick return-on-investment (ROI) analysis with the per customer numbers on the chart to arrive at the right answer.)

Interviewee: Well, in order to decide that, you'd need to calculate which type of program gives you the greatest return for the costs. For the retailer affinity cards, it looks like you get a (.45/.55=.818) 82 percent return on the program. For the airline frequent buyer cards, it looks like you get a (10/7=1.428) 143 percent return on the program. For the household cleaner rebates for frequent purchases program, it looks like you get a (3/2.5=1.2) 120 percent return. For the last one, the CPG discount coupon club, you get (10/9=1.11) a 110 percent return. On a pure cost-benefit basis in terms of sales and costs, it looks like the airline frequent buyer program is the most effective and the best one.

Firm: That's right. It does get you the highest sales life for the costs incurred running the program. But you alluded to the fact that there might be other non-quantitative benefits to each of the programs. What might those be?

(This is a more advanced question. If the interviewee is new to case interviews—or the business world in general—he or she would definitely not be expected to answer this. But a more experienced interviewee would want to be able to speak to this.)

Interviewee: Sales lifts are obviously good, but if they are only temporary, or a sign of "pantry-loading," that's not great. Any marketing effort should also be looked at in terms of branding—how much does the program increase brand awareness or loyalty? I imagine that the client wants this program to increase brand loyalty over time.

Firm: That's right. Now, look at Exhibit 1. Say that we presented this to the client—and not just the CEO, whose idea this program was, but to others at his company—as a reason why it should create a consumer loyalty program modeled after an airline frequent flyer program, what kind of "push-back" do you think we'd get from the marketing folks at the client?

(Again, this is more of an advanced question. If the interviewee is new as stated above, he or she would definitely not be expected to answer this. But a more

© 2008 Vault.com Inc.

experienced interviewee would want to be able to make an observation or two. If the interviewee can hit all of these points, it shows great awareness of the limits of pieces of data and client relationship management.)

Interviewee: I can think of a few things that people at the client company might push back on. First, each of the examples in Exhibit 1 are benchmarks from other companies, other products and even other industries. I imagine that the marketing team would say that they're not "pure comparables." I imagine that clients would want a better test of how a loyalty program would work for their company, their products and their customer target, mothers. Second, before declaring a sort of "frequent buyer program" modeled after the airline industry, which is the "best," even in terms of sales lift versus cost, I imagine they'd want to consider what kind of ROI they're getting from other types of marketing programs—both potential loyalty programs and other marketing initiatives like advertising, sampling, coupons, etc.

Firm: That's exactly right. Given that, let me show you Exhibit 2. Now, tell me what this tells you.

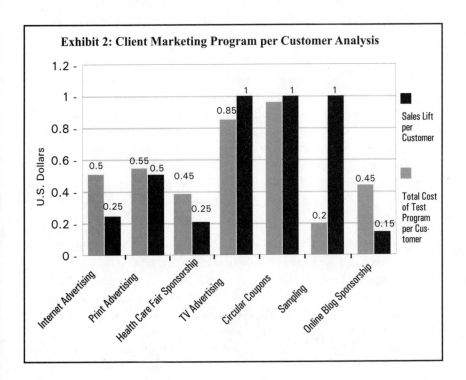

Exhibit 2: Client Marketing Program per Customer Analysis

Visit the Vault Consulting Career Channel at **www.vault.com/consulting** — with insider firm profiles, message boards, the Vault Consulting Job Board and more.

V/\ULT CAREER LIBRARY

69

Interviewee: Well, first I would calculate the ROIs for each of these marketing activities.

Firm: Don't worry about that or being so precise on this one. I know you can do the math, but just glancing at this graph, what do you see?

Interviewee: Just glancing at it, it looks like sampling, coupons and TV advertising have the worst ROIs in terms of sales lift to costs. And, it looks like Internet advertising and "online blog sponsorships" provide the best, which kind of surprises me.

Firm: That's right, and yeah, that kind of surprised us to. But we looked into it, and it seems that the direct marketing that different Internet marketing tools can provide show pretty high ROIs. In turns out that moms spend a lot of time online at home and respond pretty heavily to it. In fact, a lot of young moms are at home, dying for an online community, which the blogs in some way answer. That was new knowledge for us, but not so much for the marketing folks at the client. However, it was new knowledge for the CEO. In fact, let's get back to him. Let's say that you're at the client site and run into him in the hallway—he's very excited to find out how the case is going. What would you say to him? How would you summarize this case and what we've learned?

(This is actually a favorite case interview tactic—summarize the case to the CEO "who you run into in the hallway/elevator at the client. It's a test of how quickly and succinctly you can summarize a case interview. And interviewee should do three things: 1) summarize data/analysis done, definitely referring back to at least one number calculated; 2) state an opinion or recommendation given the analysis done—not worrying too much about whether it's right or wrong; and 3) state that the team is still working and evaluating all risks/rewards before the final presentation will be complete. It's also a little role play, which sometimes happens in case interviews, so interviewees should not be surprised.)

Interviewee: Well, in looking a various consumer loyalty benchmarks from other companies and other industries, it seems that airlines' frequent flyer programs show pretty good returns in terms of sales lift for the costs of the programs—in fact, they show a ROI of over 140 percent, which is great, and I can see why you thought this would be a good thing to look into for your company's consumers. However, when we compare this to some other types of marketing activities, which we do with our target consumers—mothers—it appears that the ROIs are even higher with some of our Internet marketing programs. It turns out that online efforts have even greater ROIs. So, for now, if we did do something for our moms—even some sort of loyalty program—we

 © 2008 Vault.com Inc.

should probably design something online, because that's where we seem to do the most for our target consumers and our company's sales.

Firm: That's great. Just quickly, what do you see as the risk of this recommendation to the CEO? Or, let me rephrase that, what might you be concerned about in recommending not to do a loyalty program like the airline frequent flyer programs?

(This is also a "nice-to-have" answer in the case interview. By no means, will every interviewee get this, but if you do, it shows real understanding of client relationships.)

Interviewee: Well, the only thing that comes to mind is that this idea that we just evaluated and declined was the CEO's idea, wasn't it? And we have a strong relationship with him, don't we? He may not like us not recommending it.

Firm: That's great. And you're right—it is a little delicate. But, I have to say, that one of the reasons why we have such a good relationship with him is that we do good, data-driven analysis and work. That's why he trusts us and hires us all the time. So, we're better off delicately shooting down his ideas if they don't make business sense than just recommending them to stay on his good side. But it's good that you recognize that we have to be a little careful about it.

That's it. Great job!

Housing Loans Market Entry Case

Your client is a U.S. bank that provides housing loans. It specializes in the subprime market. The U.S. market is becoming saturated and the bank is thinking about entering the Canadian market as a way to grow. It would provide the same services, ideally under its own brand so as not to diversify its product.

It does not know if this can be an effective growth strategy. It has asked you to help make a decision.

(This case deals with a market entry decision complicated by the new market's situation in a different country. If you think of frameworks you need to do a market analysis, and if the conclusion is favorable then possibly develop a market entry strategy as well. The first question that should come to mind is, what is the "subprime" market? You may have heard of a "prime rate," for example, which is not what is referred to in this case. Even if you have a finance background and are familiar with this term, it would be a good idea to tell the interviewer what you think it refers to just to verify that you are correct.)

Visit the Vault Consulting Career Channel at **www.vault.com/consulting** — with insider firm profiles, message boards, the Vault Consulting Job Board and more.

VAULT CAREER LIBRARY

71

Interviewee: Before starting to think about the case, I'd like to clarify what "subprime market" refers to.

Firm: Sure. The subprime market refers to customers who do not qualify for housing loans from normal lenders. This might be due to several reasons, most leading to them having a bad credit rating. They are considered a higher risk because of this poor credit rating, and many mainstream lending institutions will not give them a loan. Those that do will take on the higher risk in exchange for charging a higher lending rate, typically 3 to 4 percentage points. For banks operating in this market, there is also an element of having a sufficiently large number of borrowers; it raises your financial exposure but also diversifies your risk since the pool of people who will not default is also larger.

(Now that you understand the context better, it's time to provide a structure to analyze the case. You will probably need to ask a lot of questions to get the information you need to reach a decision. You need to think about the Canadian market's suitability to achieving the growth goal as well as the feasibility of entering a new market, particularly one that is in a different country.)

Interviewee: I would like to analyze the case on two levels. The first is to understand whether or not entering this market will help our client achieve its goal of growth. The second is to assess if the client has the ability to enter and compete in a new market that is situated in a different country.

Firm: OK, where would you like to begin?

Interviewee: I'd like to start with assessing whether or not entering the Canadian market is actually an appropriate strategy to achieve the client's goal of growth. Why did the client choose the Canadian market?

Firm: It was more Canada choosing itself than the client really choosing Canada. Growth in the U.S. was slowing down as the market became increasingly saturated. The bank looked North and South and the Canadian market had far more in its favor than the Mexican one in all aspects—potential size, similarity of financial and legal institutions, and so on, and so it chose to target Canada. It does not want to consider going outside North America at this time.

Interviewee: What is the market size and growth rate in Canada as compared to the U.S.?

Firm: The U.S. subprime market is about $150 billion with a growth rate of about 3 to 5 percent while the Canadian market is about $20 billion with growth rates of almost 20 percent over the last few years. So far the Canadian market has also shown lower rates of defaulters but this may be due to the fact that only the top end of the subprime candidates are currently being serviced.

© 2008 Vault.com Inc.

(Always remember to keep a forward-looking perspective and not just rely on historical data. A market could be in the middle of a growth bubble and on the verge of bursting, which would be the worst time to enter a market.)

Interviewee: Is this growth trend in the Canadian market expected to continue at similar rates?

Firm: It may not maintain 20 percent growth but it is expected to grow in the double digits for the next few years.

Interviewee: OK, so the market itself is definitely growing at a faster rate than in the U.S. If the client was able to establish profitable operations that grew at least at the same pace as market, then it would achieve its objective of growing faster than it would by staying only in the U.S. market. I'd like to move to the second part of the analysis to assess the feasibility of entering and competing in the market. I'd like to analyze the market in terms of incumbents, customers and entry barriers.

*(It is important to mention "**profitable** operations." No one wants to grow revenue at a fast rate but have an overall profit decline for too long (initial losses are commonplace when establishing new operations). It's good to further refine your structure as you move through the case and determine what is required.)*

Firm: That sounds reasonable.

Interviewee: Beginning with the incumbents, is the industry currently fragmented with several players or is it more of a monopoly or oligopoly structure?

Firm: The market has an oligopoly structure. It mainly consists of the five major banks that are starting to provide this service or have affiliates doing it for them. These five banks operate nationally and dominate the market with a very high percentage of all financial business across Canada.

(In a highly consolidated market with big players, market share can be tough for a new entrant but there are a few different strategies. Here is an opportunity to be creative. Pick two or three that you think are the best and outline them.)

Interviewee: It seems like the market is relatively consolidated and the incumbents are big players with deep pockets. Nevertheless there might be a few different ways the client could enter the market. For example it could come into the market in a big way by buying out one of the incumbents and taking over the business, of course this could be quite expensive. Another option could be to enter with an offering that is highly differentiated either in terms of the product itself or the customer service aspect, that will successfully attract customers away from the incumbents.

Visit the Vault Consulting Career Channel at **www.vault.com/consulting** — with insider firm profiles, message boards, the Vault Consulting Job Board and more.

VAULT CAREER LIBRARY

73

Firm: The second option is more interesting but also limited, given that this is a major, usually once-in-a-lifetime investment that people make, and risk management, legal and other requirements allow limited room for creativity in structuring the loan. The client could make some changes to the standard product and service that might attract people, but how will it bring these to market? The first option of buying an incumbent is far too expensive.

Interviewee: Even with the second option, the client will still need a physical presence in the country. If a local incumbent's operations cannot be taken over, the entrant has to either establish its own operations or alternatively have a joint venture with one of the incumbents.

Firm: Let's explore these two options further.

(Recognize that you are well and truly in the middle of a "deep dive." The interviewer is pushing you to go beyond just high-level assumptions and steps, hence you should tailor your answers accordingly.)

Interviewee: If the competition consists of the big five banks who are dominant nationally, setting up its own network that can compete with these would be quite expensive and would not be a fast process. We could, however, approach the problem by targeting one region at a time.

Firm: How would you do this?

Interviewee: I would try to use the customer analysis to develop a ranking to prioritize the different regions.

Firm: What kind of customer analysis are you thinking of?

Interviewee: Since we are planning to offer the same basic product in Canada, I am assuming the customer profile we would target there is very similar to the one in the U.S.

Firm: Yes, that is a reasonable assumption.

Interviewee: Do we have details of this customer profile or market data for where they are concentrated geographically in Canada?

Firm: We don't have any geographic-based demographic data right now. Is there any proxy you can use?

(The interviewer is guiding you to make some high-level assumptions to move on. Determining and using a proxy for actual data is very common for consultants to do early in the process of a case when good data is not available [or to move ahead while they are waiting for the data to arrive, for example the results of a survey] and it is a skill that you can develop with practice. Try to think

of any previous information that might help you choose a proxy. State your assumption and, if the interviewer agrees, move ahead with it.)

Interviewee: In general, any profile type is probably more likely to appear in greater numbers closer to the main population centers of Canada. I am also thinking about the earlier information that this business can be about volume, where you need a large pool of borrowers to diversify the risk of defaulters. So, as a very rough first proxy, I would think about the main population centers of Canada and would apply metrics to rank them.

Firm: Could you clarify that please? What kind of metrics are you thinking of?

Interviewee: For example, I would look at density of population. We are not yet sure how many physical locations we would have, but regardless we would want to be in areas where a single location could serve the maximum number of people. Another metric could be to try and match community profiles to those that we target in the U.S. so that we are close to communities that have the customer profile that forms our customer base.

Firm: So you are suggesting a customer analysis that will look at size and density of population and then community profile to prioritize locations to enter the market.

Interviewee: Yes. I would probably look at cities or groups of cities as the analysis unit.

Firm: Let's simplify and assume the province of Ontario has the most number of cities that rank highly in this analysis, what should the client do next?

(Reassess where you are so far in the structure you proposed. Do not hesitate to do this out loud as interviewers gain an insight into how you are thinking. It also shows that you are using the structure you had proposed earlier and did not just forget about it.)

Interviewee: We were assessing how to enter the market and were looking at the option where the client enters with a differentiated product on its own but does so in a gradual manner, one region at a time to keep its market entry costs manageable. So far we have determined a metric for choosing where to enter but still need to think about how to enter. In my earlier structure, I talked about looking at incumbents, customers and entry barriers. I'd like to look at the last one now. Are there any legal or regulatory barriers to entry by a foreign bank in this sector of the economy?

Firm: No, assume there are no such barriers. So are you recommending the client should try to enter the market in the regions identified?

(Don't forget there was a second option to be explored. It will reflect very poorly if you do. You might be able to use some of the information you have already deduced.)

Interviewee: Before reaching a recommendation, I also want to look at the second entry option identified, which was to come in through a joint venture.

Firm: Sure. How would we go about doing this?

Interviewee: I think the customer analysis can be reused over here to help us think about locations to enter the market. Assuming we can find an appropriate partner, entering through a joint venture is likely to be less expensive and might allow us to enter the market in a more widespread manner than if we acted alone.

Firm: So how would you decide between these two options?

Interviewee: I think I need more information to choose between the two options. For the first option, I'd like to understand what would be the financial costs of setting up independent operations—acquiring locations, hiring staff, marketing and so on, and develop this over a three- or five-year plan tied in with how many locations we think we might open. Apart from the costs, I'd look at the revenue side to determine break even requirements and profit margins that can be expected. For the second option, I would also do the cost and profit analysis keeping in mind that some of the costs, such as marketing, might be shared but so would profits. Again I would develop this over a time period of a few years tied with the geographic spread that we could achieve by entering through a partnership. Simultaneously, I also need to assess the feasibility of finding an appropriate joint venture partner and having such partner agree to a favorable contract. If the five big banks are the only possible partners in this market, it's possible that none of them are interested in entering into a partnership, which may mean there is only one real option available.

Firm: Could you close the case by wrapping up your recommendations?

Interviewee: I would recommend to the client that there is the potential to meet the growth objective by entering the Canadian market since it is growing at a faster rate that the U.S. market and is expected to do so in the near future. The main question is since they are moving into a new country—it needs to decide the best way it should enter—either independently but in a slower manner or through a joint venture and more broadly if it can find a suitable joint

© 2008 Vault.com Inc.

venture partner. The decision may actually be quite obvious once we do the analysis I just described for both options.

Firm: Thank you.

Case analysis

This case has two parts. The first is a market analysis and the second is a market entry decision. Of course, the second part is only required if the market analysis indicates that entering the Canadian market might help achieve the growth objective identified by the company. If you jumped straight to the operational part of things, you may be doing a lot of work that is ultimately useless for your client.

The interviewer moved into some depth and, as mentioned in the case, you need to recognize when the interviewer has guided you into a deep dive and adapt to it to show you can go beyond just skimming the surface of issues. The case could have also become more quantitative if the interviewer brought up market sizing figures and cost and revenue numbers; you should be prepared for the interviewer to bring out charts or tables to introduce this data.

IT Benchmarking and Business Alignment Case

A new CIO has just been hired by a large automotive manufacturer (or in industry parlance, OEM—original equipment manufacturer). The CIO has asked several consulting firms to perform a benchmarking study to provide insight into how this manufacturer compares to its primary competitors—specifically, in terms of how IT investment is being used to improve key business processes.

You have been assigned to the project team for your firm, and you have a meeting with a member of the CIO's staff to plan your firm's approach. Share with her how you plan to structure and perform the benchmarking study.

Interviewee: Our firm is pleased to have been invited to perform the benchmarking study for you, and I am eager to find out more about what you have in mind. Since time is always an important factor, let's start with your expectations of the duration of the study.

Firm: We are expecting a final report approximately six weeks from today, with an interim progress report for the CIO during the fourth week and a final presentation to the CIO's staff in week six or seven, schedules permitting.

Visit the Vault Consulting Career Channel at **www.vault.com/consulting** — with insider firm profiles, message boards, the Vault Consulting Job Board and more.

VAULT CAREER LIBRARY   77

(You have now verified the time horizon for the study.)

Interviewee: A benchmarking study will typically gather a potentially large amount of data. Once we determine the most important areas we need to explore, will subject matter experts within your company be available to help us establish some baseline data about the company?

Firm: We expect the benchmarking study to be performed based on primary sources from within each consulting firm's auto practice and from secondary, publicly available research. IT and business trends in the auto industry tend to be covered quite heavily by the media. We feel comfortable that an insightful study is feasible, even if based on secondary research and the insights of your firm's experience in the automotive industry. So we consider input from our operating executives to be outside the scope of the study.

(Now you have determined the client's expectation as to the sources of data, and the process by which you'll gather it.)

Interviewee: Now that we have clarified the duration and expected sources of data, who do you consider to be your primary competitors?

Firm: Including this company, there are six major players of interest—i.e., companies A through F.

Interviewee: What are the key business process areas of interest?

Firm: Product development, manufacturing, supply chain and customer experience.

(The named competitors and the primary business process areas to be targeted by the study are now confirmed.)

Interviewee: Before we go further, can you share with me the intended use of this study by your CIO?

Firm: My boss, the CIO, has a mandate from the board to accomplish the following objectives: 1) reduce overall spending on IT, and 2) improve the effectiveness of IT in supporting the business.

Interviewee: Is there a numerical target for spend reduction?

Firm: The metric we are using is to reach an IT spend amount that is approximately 1.25 percent of revenue.

Interviewee: What is the percentage of revenue today?

Firm: Roughly 1.75 percent.

© 2008 Vault.com Inc.

Interviewee: Let's look at the allocation of IT spending to each of the targeted business process areas—is this information readily available?

Firm: Twenty percent of IT spending occurs in product development; manufacturing consumes 30 percent; supply consumes 10 percent, and customer experience consumes 20 percent. The remaining 20 percent is spent on other process areas and infrastructure.

Interviewee: Thanks very much for this baseline. Later in the study, I'll need to know about recent trends (i.e., increasing, decreasing or flat) but I'll come back to that after we establish a data-gathering framework that makes sense for you and your competitors.

(The personal objectives of the CIO are now confirmed, as is the relative amount and share of overall IT spend consumed by each of the targeted process areas. The degree of expected reduction is also known, which in turn provides a needed framework for the data you'll collect on the group of competitors as a whole.)

Interviewee: The CIO's objectives are obviously driven by the needs of the business—can you share with me what enterprise-level challenges may be driving his agenda?

Firm: The search for cost reduction opportunities is pretty much a fact of life in the auto industry. A firm of this size spends a lot on IT, and therefore our investment in information technology is always a target for cost reduction.

Interviewee: How is IT valued within the business process areas we are targeting?

Firm: The executives who lead the respective process areas have come to rely on technology as a way to improve productivity, but they have historically had a difficult time quantifying its value. They know they need it, but they have a tough time justifying the spending level.

Interviewee: At the highest level, any investment needs to produce a return to the business. So how is the return on IT investment determined in your current environment?

Firm: We evaluate IT investment from two perspectives. The first is the degree to which any given initiative will contribute to operating cost reduction. The second is the degree to which an initiative has the potential to contribute to revenue growth.

Visit the Vault Consulting Career Channel at **www.vault.com/consulting** — with insider firm profiles, message boards, the Vault Consulting Job Board and more.

V/\ULT CAREER LIBRARY   **79**

Interviewee: How much importance do the operating executives (i.e., the internal customers of the CIO) attach to the IT strategies being implemented by their competitors?

Firm: It's very important—creating a reputation for innovative use of technology is not only important internally to improve processes, it is vitally important as a marketing image to the car-buying public.

(The objectives driving the CIO's motivation to perform the study are identified, the context of the enterprise view of IT is now known, and the way this company evaluates IT initiatives has been established.)

Interviewee: Let's look at the business process areas in a bit more detail. What is the primary challenge in the area of product development?

Firm: Reduced time-to-market, i.e., bringing new products to market in a shorter amount of time.

Interviewee: Since time-to-market is such an important aspect, what metrics are being used to define the improvement you hope to achieve?

Firm: Our assumption is that our investment in IT will result in a minimum reduction in time-to-market for a vehicle program of 12 weeks. Once our processes have taken full advantage of the IT, we expect additional improvement of between 26 and 52 weeks.

Interviewee: At a high level, what is the recent history of IT investment in the product development area?

Firm: We have just completed a round of massive investments in the deployment of advanced software tools and the infrastructure necessary to support global product development.

Interviewee: What results have been achieved to date, based on the 20 percent of overall IT spend going into this area?

Firm: It's a bit early to tell, since the tools have only recently been implemented. But we believe our goals are achievable.

(You have quantified the amount of improvement the business expects to gain from its IT investment in the product development area. In addition, you have established that the bulk of investment is behind them, and that benefit realization is yet to be achieved.)

Interviewee: What is the primary manufacturing challenge?

© 2008 Vault.com Inc.

Firm: Labor cost per vehicle—therefore, we continue to invest mainly in automated assembly and material handling technology.

Interviewee: Given the 30 percent of IT spend in this area, what results have been achieved to date?

Firm: We are on track to achieve our goal of a 20 percent reduction in labor content/car within 24 months.

Interviewee: Moving forward, what is the likely IT spend trajectory, i.e. increasing, decreasing or flat?

Firm: Given the pressure to reduce IT as a category, we expect to have to adjust to lower spending in IT.

(Based on the insights your client shared with you regarding the product development and manufacturing areas, you are now able to conclude that each process area is likely to have its own unique performance measurement parameters. In addition, you now have enough high-level structure to describe what some of the deliverables will look like.)

Interviewee: Thanks very much for your guidance so far. Now that we've discussed the high-level product development and manufacturing process areas, a pattern is beginning to emerge that I believe will facilitate our data gathering, and also show you where your company is compared to others.

Business performance parameters will vary by process within each OEM. Our approach will include observing the parameters each OEM uses within its respective business processes, then developing a ranked, normalized matrix designed to generate insights for the study. Again, the performance parameters in each area will vary. Therefore, we will begin to construct frameworks for gathering data, ultimately providing you with comparative insights regarding your competitors. We will create a series of charts depicting the relative strength of each process area by competitor, and also the importance of IT as a factor in contributing to the relative strength of each competitor's ranking. As we proceed, we will come back to establish appropriate frameworks for the supply chain and customer experience process areas. Are exhibits of this nature in line with your expectations of the deliverables of the study?

Firm: Yes, I think you are on the right track.

Interviewee: What are you doing right now to achieve IT cost reduction?

Firm: We are trying to give more volume to fewer suppliers, with the expectation that our costs will be reduced by leveraging increased volume and longer-term contracts.

Interviewee: Let's examine the IT supplier perspective. Can you tell me who your primary suppliers are, and what relative share of your overall IT investment goes to each?

Firm: We are heavily outsourced; so at present, 70 percent of our IT spend goes to one supplier.

Interviewee: How many suppliers comprise the remaining IT expenditures?

Firm: The major players are all represented, varying by business process area—they consume 20 percent of the spending, and 10 percent of the spending is allocated to our CIO's organization.

Interviewee: Do you have a preconceived strategy as to how the current spending with your current dominant supplier will be reallocated?

Firm: We feel we will need to assess the relative strengths of our IT suppliers in terms of their ability to support our business process areas on a global basis. Our hope is that the benchmarking study will provide some initial insights as to what these suppliers have been able to deliver to our competitors, and the results they have achieved. This will serve as a potential model for reallocating our IT expenditures to a more diverse supplier base.

Interviewee: The importance of IT investment as a driver of relative business process strength is clear, and I believe the study will produce significant insights in this area. During the course of the study, it may also be important to identify any "best practice" IT strategies or initiatives that leading firms are pursuing. Do you wish to know what these are?

Firm: Definitely. Any relevant insights your study can produce that may give us a different perspective will be considered valuable.

(You now have a perspective of the current allocation of IT spend to the suppliers, and what rationale your client intends to use to reallocate the mix of spending among them.

At this point, you have quantified the clients' expectations for the study methodology, the data to be gathered, the time frame for completion and the insights the client hopes to gain from the study. In addition, you have gained high-level validation from the client as to the usefulness of some of the primary deliverable frameworks you have in mind. You are now sufficiently prepared to begin the engagement.)

© 2008 Vault.com Inc.

IT Outsourcing Strategy Case

Your client, ABC Corp., a large information technology outsourcing service provider, is nearing the end of a long-term contract with its largest customer. The customer has notified ABC of its intent to "level the playing field" of competition for its IT-related business. The customer has indicated that 100 percent of the business ABC currently enjoys will be available for bids by ABC's competitors. In addition, the customer has announced that the bidding will be structured within a series of standardized service offering categories. Although ABC has detailed information regarding its many individual contracts with the various business units of its customer, it has a very poor overall sense of the mix of services it provides to each customer unit. ABC would like your assistance in developing a view of its business with this customer, oriented around the standardized service offerings the customer is likely to specify. In addition, ABC believes the trend to structure outsourcing initiatives by standardized service lines will continue, and therefore it views this client opportunity as a "wave of the future" that it will soon see repeated with its other major clients. ABC ultimately desires to have a fact-based perspective on which of its service offerings are winners, losers or somewhere in between, so as to be able to make informed decisions about where it should invest, divest or "stay the course."

You have been assigned to the project team for your firm, and you have a meeting with ABC's executive-in-charge for this client account. Your desired outcome is to understand ABC's situation as the company perceives it in greater detail, to develop a high-level engagement approach and to do some initial brainstorming as to what insights are needed to strengthen ABC's response to the forthcoming bid process.

Interviewee: Our firm is pleased to have been invited to contribute to your effort to retain or grow this important piece of business. First of all, what are the critical calendar milestones we need to be aware of, so that we ensure the results of this project can be put into play as effectively as possible?

Firm: We have eight months until the start of negotiations with our customer, but we need to have our strategy nailed down internally within five months, to allow for various review cycles with our C-level executives and, potentially, with the board of directors.

Interviewee: I would like to understand a little more about how much risk you realistically think you face in the upcoming negotiations with your customer. Have any assumptions or analyses been developed to help you quantify just how much you stand to lose?

Firm: We are anticipating losing a certain amount of business, and we are looking to this project to help us quantify the risk to a granular level, and thus be able to justify whatever actions we take. Our operating assumption right now is that our loss exposure to competitors ranges between 10 and 25 percent.

Interviewee: Have you identified the key factors likely to drive the outcome, and if so, which ones can you influence most?

Firm: Aside from obvious factors such as unit price benchmarking and service level definitions, we believe our customer will have significant switching costs in certain areas, which could work in our favor. Therefore, in mission-critical areas, we believe our customer may be reluctant to divert its business with us to one or more competitors en masse.

(You have now confirmed with your client that unit pricing, service level definition and switching costs are key factors that need to be considered within the analytical phase of the project.)

Interviewee: Do you have a sense of the parts of your business that face the most risk?

Firm: Please clarify what you mean.

Interviewee: Either by customer business unit or by the service lines you offer, does your leadership team have a sense of which units or service lines are most at risk?

Firm: This is among the insights we are expecting to gain from this project.

(You also now know that significant work must be done to create a sensitivity analysis of, at minimum, where the risk lies by customer business unit and by the major service lines your client delivers.)

Interviewee: We will no doubt dive deeper into this later, but it's important at the start to understand the basics. Can you share with me some specific, yet basic details of what this business looks like?

Firm: Our master service agreement with this customer today breaks down into a series of 10 individual service contracts, which closely align with the way the customer's profit centers are organized. From an individual delivery perspective, most or all of the IT services provided by ABC are consumed to one degree or another, by these contracts.

Interviewee: What is the nature of the services you provide, and how are they organized?

© 2008 Vault.com Inc.

Firm: We provide many different services to each of the 10 business units. Although some of these services are standardized across our company, and are delivered by our infrastructure delivery organization, we need to look closely at all of these offerings to see if common denominators exist that will support some level of consolidation.

Interviewee: For the standardized services, do you have metrics in place that enable you to see profit and loss by service line, across the customer's business units?

Firm: For the standardized offerings, we have fairly reliable data. Regarding the "cats and dogs" services that vary significantly from business unit to business unit, we are looking to this project to provide some insight.

(You have now quantified the number of business units. In addition, you know that although some of the services you will be analyzing are standardized across the customer's business units, potentially many others are not. This allows you to develop a set of assumptions about the tasks and deliverables that will need to be part of the project.)

Interviewee: Who do you consider to be your primary competitors?

Firm: Based on our competitive experience in other markets, as well as with the occasional competitive bidding we have seen with our customer to date, we believe the most significant competition will come from competitors A through D.

Interviewee: Do you have some sense of which aspects of your customer's business these companies will attack?

Firm: Only at a very high level. We are looking to this project to give us a greater sense of who we will face across the dimensions of our customer's organization, major processes and our service lines.

Interviewee: I think we are getting close to understanding the landscape of where you are today, the challenges you face and the kind of analyses needed to give you the insights to best manage the decision process that lies ahead. Let's discuss the process by which we can work with your team to begin this project. Have you identified who from your organization should work on this with us?

Firm: I agree. I plan to ask each member of my staff to appoint someone from within their respective organizations to commit to work on this project on a largely full-time basis, as needed.

Interviewee: I suggest that we have someone who understands the financial structure of the business, and who has strong relationships with the people who are managing delivery of the services.

Firm: Agreed.

Interviewee: I also propose that we create an executive oversight group, whose function will be to ensure that the priorities are set, and that key resources are allocated to the project as needed to drive the analysis.

Firm: As you decide how best to conduct this analysis, please keep in mind the fact that the very same people who have the knowledge we need to tap are also the ones running the business on a day-to-day basis. Will you be able to estimate the time commitment our people will need to plan for?

Interviewee: Absolutely. Based on this discussion today, I am confident we will be able to return to you shortly with a more detailed approach and some concepts illustrating the deliverables we will create.

(You have now established a framework for project organization and governance.)

Firm: Can you share with me what some of these deliverables might look like?

Interviewee: Definitely. Based on the discussion we have had, I propose we develop a series of charts and graphs that characterize the footprint of the services you deliver to this client today. Before we consider what it will take to assess how these services stack up against likely competitive actions, we will look at your customer's business strategy and direction. This will give us insight as to where growth opportunities may exist for us to focus on as we gather data to support the analysis. In planning our defense of your current business, we do not want to lose sight of opportunities that may arise to help your customer achieve their business objectives. Once we have a first look at these, we will develop hypotheses about the basis for competitiveness by service line, by your customer's business unit, and by likely competitive actions. In some cases, the facts we get from your organization will be very solid. In cases where the data is soft, we will develop various indices to fill in the gaps. In any case, we will keep your team, the guidance group and your staff informed throughout the process. Does this sound like we are in agreement and you can feel comfortable we are off to a strong start?

Firm: Yes. What do you think we need to do to get started?

Interviewee: I will prepare a few pages on our discussion today. These pages will describe the project charter, organization, goals, illustrative deliverables and the process we will use to create the deliverables. In addition, I will provide a major task list, timeline for completion and preliminary list of participants identifying all contributors and stakeholders.

© 2008 Vault.com Inc.

(At this point, you have identified the client's current situation, the desired outcomes of the project at a high level, and the process you will use to ensure effective project execution. In addition, you have gained high-level validation from the client as to how useful are some of the primary deliverable frameworks you have in mind, and the time frame required. You are now sufficiently prepared to begin the engagement.)

Medical Devices Case

Our consulting firm has been hired. The client is very profitable and doing well. In fact, its business has grown from a small, regional medical supplies manufacturer and distributor with annual sales of $100 million ten years ago to having annual sales of $2 billion today. However, it's not sure that all of this fast growth has been great. In fact, it knows it hasn't: it knows that its margins have decreased. It has hired us to explain why that is, but in the end we told it more than that.

Additional information provided during questioning

• The company makes medical supplies. While the product itself is not a focal point for the case, if the interviewee asks, the interviewer will tell them that the company makes products like surgical packs with clean surgical tools, syringes, swabs, gloves, etc.

• The company started out with a small product line-cotton swabs, hygienic swipes and medicated tissues were the basis of its product line. It has expanded tremendously to include disposable surgical clothing, surgical packs with sterile tools, syringes, plastic containers for blood and other bodily fluids, etc.

• The company was a small regional player in the South of the United States originally. Now, it serves all 50 states and some hospitals in Canada and Mexico.

• The company's customers are primarily hospitals and hospital chains, but it also serves some large physician group practices and clinics, depending on the regional area.

This is a profitability case, but it moves quickly from the profitability framework to data analysis, brainstorming and problem solving. While the client does want the firm to answer the question about why profitability has declined, the interviewer will likely hint up front that the interviewee should push even further to fixing the problem.

Visit the Vault Consulting Career Channel at **www.vault.com/consulting** – with insider firm profiles, message boards, the Vault Consulting Job Board and more.

VΛULT CAREER LIBRARY   **87**

This is a good case for practicing looking at data and brainstorming different causes for the resulting data. It also is a great example of how an interviewee can take a case past just structuring and solving the question to actually trying to "fix" the problem and implement a solution, which is what some firms are looking for.

Breakdown of solution (including quantitative analyses and qualitative evaluations)

Firm: First, do you have any questions?

Interviewee: Yes, I want to make sure that I understand how the client's business works. You said that it was a small, regional manufacturer and distributor of medical supplies. What kind of supplies does it make?

Firm: Sure, that makes sense. It makes products like surgical packs with clean surgical tools, syringes, swabs, gloves, etc. The company started out with a small product line—cotton swabs, hygienic swipes and medicated tissues were the basis of its product line. It has expanded tremendously to include disposable surgical clothing, surgical packs with sterile tools, syringes, plastic containers for blood and other bodily fluids, etc.

Interviewee: Great. And I'm assuming that we're focused only on the U.S. market—or should I consider other markets as well?

Firm: The company was a small regional player in the South of the United States originally. Now it serves all 50 states and some hospitals in Canada and Mexico. But, for the purposes of this case, just focus on the U.S.

Interviewee: And before I get started, can you just give me a sense of who its customers are? I mean, does it market to physicians like pharma companies do, or to someone else?

(One thing that's great to do during this initial questioning is to drive some of the descriptions. For example, even though the interviewee would really just like to know who the customers are, he/she throws in comparables—pharma companies. It shows the interviewee's knowledge of the industry and use of comparables.)

Firm: That's a great question. The company's customers are primarily hospitals and hospital chains, but it also serves some large physician group practices and clinics, depending on the regional area. Does that give you the sense that you were looking for?

Interviewee: Yeah, that's great. And just so I'm clear on the client's question: It has seen its profitability decline as the company has grown, and it's just curious as to why and how to reverse that trend?

© 2008 Vault.com Inc.

Firm: That's right—now, how would you try to answer that question? Feel free to take a few minutes to collect your thoughts.

Interviewee: Great—thanks.

(A few minutes go by...)

Interviewee: I would want to look at the two levers of profitability—revenue and costs—to understand whether there have been changes on either side that might have led to eroding profitability. I'd like to start on the costs side, as I'm wondering if while the company has grown, it's had to incur some costs due to expansion that has made it less profitable.

(The structure for the case is spot on. But because profitability cases are so easy and clear to structure, it's a good idea to suggest which lever you'd like to look into and your hypothesis as to why that might lead to the answer—it shows that you are really driving the case.)

Firm: That's great. And we actually looked at expansion in its cost base as it grew—and the C suite of the client had looked at that, too—but that's not where the answer actually lies. The client had kept a good eye on its costs—and its cost base—so, that's actually not where the answer is, but it's a good hunch. After we eliminated costs, that left revenue. What would you look at there?

Interviewee: Well, revenue is price times units. Since its business has grown in terms of regions and customers, I'm going to assume that units sold has increased. Has anything changed in terms of price? Has it gone down?

Firm: That's right on track. Let me show you some data that we collected on the discounts that it's giving to its customers. What does this data tell you?

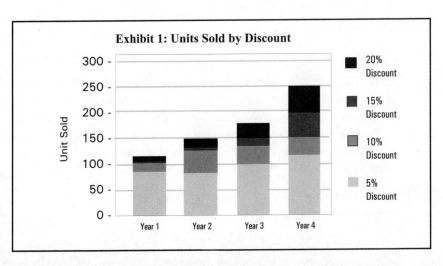

Exhibit 1: Units Sold by Discount

Visit the Vault Consulting Career Channel at **www.vault.com/consulting** — with insider firm profiles, message boards, the Vault Consulting Job Board and more.

VAULT CAREER LIBRARY   **89**

Interviewee: Well, it looks like the number of units sold under a higher discount has grown over the years. In Year 1, it looks like 120 units were sold in total, and about 110 of those were sold at a five to 10 percent discount. Whereas, in Year 4, it looks like the number of units sold grew to 250, but only almost 150 of those were sold at a five to 10 percent discount.

Firm: So, what percent were sold at the higher discount in Year 1 vs. Year 4?

Interviewee: Well, in Year 1, it looks like (10/120=8.3 percent) 8.3 percent were sold at the higher discount, and in Year 4, it looks like (150/250=60 percent) 60 percent were sold at the higher discount. So, they're discounting higher on more of their sales, which is why its profitability is eroding.

Firm: That's right. Now, let me show you another piece of data. What does that data tell you?

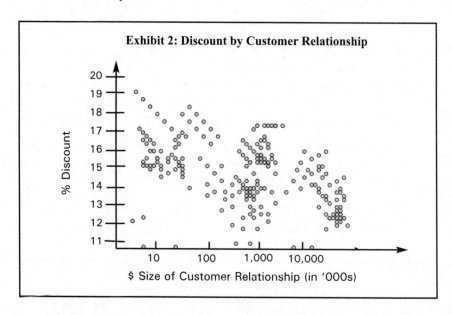

Exhibit 2: Discount by Customer Relationship

Interviewee: Well, it's not what I would expect. It looks like the company is giving some of the highest discounts on its fees to its midsized and small customers, not to its largest ones. This may be keeping the profitability high on its large clients, but it's probably destroying margins on its midsized clients, and bringing down its overall fee average. I think this shows the answer to the client's question.

Firm: Sure. Now here's another question: if you were the client, what would you want to see here?

(Here, the interviewee should generate an idea or two—maybe even draw on the exhibit to illustrate his or her point. There are three ideas below.)

Interviewee: Well, I would want to see a few things. First, I would want to be giving the biggest discounts, or the most discounts, to my larger clients—like volume discounting. Here, it doesn't look like the client is doing that—in fact, it looks like it's doing the reverse. Second, it seems pretty random where the discounts are given—I wonder what is driving them. There are a few clusters of discounts by relationship size, or even by discount size—I wonder whether the clusters of discounts represent a certain salesman, a certain region a or a certain client type, like hospital or clinic or hospital chain.

Firm: That's great. We went over this data and looked into the clusters specifically, and it turns out that there's high variation to discounting by sales person, and that this correlates to regional area. It turns out that salesmen in the South, where the company was founded, were giving much lower discounts to their clients than say salesmen in other regions, where the company was expanding into. Knowing that, how might you try to fix the problem?

Interviewee: I would make sure that all of sales force incentives were tied to low discounting, as well as revenue targets, which I think sale force members are usually incented on.

Firm: Yep—incentives are good, and we definitely recommended that to the client. But incentives are hard to change overnight, because they're in people's contracts; they often need a year to take effect after you put them in place, because it takes a while for people to adjust business practices. What else would you do?

(Here, the interviewer is testing the interviewee to come up with more solutions—it's a creative/short brainstorming test.)

Interviewee: I might also share this new data with the sales force in some sort of training so that they can see how they're affecting company's profitability— I mean, they're probably not aware that they're doing this as a whole.

Firm: That's right—train them. Now, what else?

Interviewee: I might make a companywide discount cap. Does it have that right now? I mean, in Year 1, it looked like most sales didn't go over a 10 percent discount, but by Year 3, 20 percent seemed to be the cap. Maybe the company would like to set a cap at 15 percent—or at least figure out a cap that made sense for its profitability target.

Firm: Yup. That's great, and that's exactly what we suggested.

Visit the Vault Consulting Career Channel at **www.vault.com/consulting** — with insider firm profiles, message boards, the Vault Consulting Job Board and more.

VAULT CAREER LIBRARY   91

NGO Partnership Case

Your client is a global multinational involved in a one-year-old partnership with an NGO operating in several countries. At the time the agreement was signed, the partnership was defined only at a very high level, and despite best intentions, there has been no progress, leading to frustration on both ends. Both sides have now agreed to try to launch something in a developing country where they both operate.

You have been asked to work with both organizations to understand how this partnership can progress, and whether or not this NGO is even an appropriate partnership for your client. What do you do?

From the beginning, you should realize that you have been described a situation but have been given very little information about either of the two main stakeholders—your client and the NGO. Your first goal should be to understand them.

Interviewee: I would first like to understand the different stakeholders involved. Could you tell me about our client? What businesses does it operate in?

Firm: The client is involved in international ground and air logistics as well as mail services in several countries. Its annual revenue is over $10 billion.

Interviewee: Could you also tell me about the NGO it's partnered with? What kind of work is it involved in?

Firm: The NGO is also quite large and is involved in various kinds of development work. It runs education programs, grassroots-level development work, and advises developing governments on things like social policy.

(You now know a little bit about the stakeholders involved. If you have some paper you should have noted down those activities. You also want to learn about the partnership. Understanding what it is about may help you later in making an assessment about whether the NGO is an appropriate partner for your client.)

Interviewee: I now understand a little bit about our client and its partner. Could you tell me about the partnership itself?

Firm: What would you like to know?

Interviewee: Why did both groups enter into this partnership to begin with?

Firm: The client wanted to get involved with an NGO for several reasons. A positive image in this area is becoming important because of increasing media

© 2008 Vault.com Inc.

and consumer attention to CSR—corporate social responsibility. It chose this NGO because of its global reach. Being a global company itself, it was looking for a partnership that could be visible in several different parts of the world. It did not want to just give money to fix a building or paint a classroom; it prefers to use its expertise to do something unique. It wanted a large and stable NGO so that projects could be sustained over a significant period of time and it wasn't looking for new projects or partners every few months.

As far as the NGO is concerned, it's always looking for private sector partners to support its work, either financially or in kind. It partners with all kinds and sizes of companies but was attracted in this case for very similar reasons—that is, a successful partnership with a global company could lead to work in different parts its their world.

(You learned a lot of information in that answer. CSR is important to the company not just because it is a good thing to do, but because the company wants to use it to enhance its corporate image—i.e., possible use of any results for marketing purposes. Also, the typical solutions of monetary donations or building a classroom may not appeal because they are not unique. Both parties are interested in taking advantage of each other's size and trying to launch something that can be duplicated in different parts of the world. This also means the company is going to have to look for similarly large partners if it decides this NGO is not the right one to partner with. By now you have a lot of interesting background information and should start analyzing what should happen going forward. Present a structure for how you plan to work through this analysis.)

Interviewee: I think I understand some of the context of the current situation. I would like to continue, using the following structure. I would first like to see if there are opportunities to develop this partnership, keeping in mind some of the goals of both organizations. If we determine there are no significant opportunities, I would try to evaluate if the client should consider dissolving its partnership with the NGO.

Firm: OK, that's fine.

Interviewee: Opportunities to develop this partnership can come from our client either becoming involved in the NGO's ongoing programs or working to develop something new.

Firm: I do not think the client's first choice would be to piggyback on an existing program. The NGO would also not be averse to something new, but it would need to be very much in line with what it does.

Visit the Vault Consulting Career Channel at **www.vault.com/consulting** — with insider firm profiles, message boards, the Vault Consulting Job Board and more.

V∧ULT CAREER LIBRARY   **93**

(Your interviewer is guiding you to explore opportunities for a new program. Another hint is that the NGO is likely to be more limited than the client on what it is willing to work on. This could help narrow your areas of exploration.)

Interviewee: I would like to focus on the NGO. You mentioned a few areas it works in. Could you be more specific so that I can better understand its work?

Firm: Sure. In education the NGO runs several campaigns, both independently and with the government. These can be about almost anything. In terms of development, it works in rural areas—building classrooms, clinics, transportation and communication networks, etc. Often it involves private sector partners to provide experts to implement the projects. Its work also usually involves the local or state government, either in implementation or to gain the necessary approvals. It also may advise governments on development or social policy but not actually become involved in carrying it out. When they work with governments, it is often because the government has invited them, but on occasion they will proactively develop proposals for consideration as well.

(OK, pause. You had earlier been given a hint that you may need to focus on the activities of the NGO to search for opportunities for cooperation. You have now been given a lot of information about these activities and should see if there is anything that stands out in the context of the client's core competencies. Part of your work as a consultant will be to sift through vast amounts of information to determine if any of it is useful. Do not hesitate to ask the interviewer for a few minutes to do this kind of analysis.)

Interviewee: That's a significant amount of information. I'd like to take a minute to review it and see if it suggests avenues to explore further.

Firm: Sure.

(There are several combinations that can be explored here, and in a real project it is quite likely you would explore most of them. However, the one that should stand out is the NGO's work in transportation networks [given that the client is involved in logistics]. A weaker possibility is the NGO's work in communication or education—this can be paired with the client's expertise from its mail business. It is better to identify two or three possibilities rather than just one, in case your interviewer wants to explore different alternatives.)

Interviewee: I feel there may be a few different areas to explore. One that stands out to me is the combination of the NGO's work in transportation and the client's expertise in logistics. Another potential area may be in pairing the NGO's work in communication or education with the client's mail business. I would like to explore these further.

© 2008 Vault.com Inc.

Firm: I think that's reasonable.

Interviewee: I would like to start with the first one. In the country selected, is there any transportation work that the NGO is involved in?

Firm: No, not presently. But it has periodically worked with the government in this area. The country is quite prone to hurricanes, but being a developing nation, often needs international aid to help recover. The NGO has in the past coordinated efforts at international ports in the aftermath of a hurricane. There were still lots of problems, but the NGO helped a lot.

(The interviewer has given you a specific example of the NGO's work in the country and in an area the client may be able to work in. This is likely a sign that you are on the right track and the interviewer may want you to develop it further. You could suggest this as an initial hypothesis to gauge how the interviewer wants to proceed. If the interviewer responds vaguely, you may need to consider switching tracks)

Interviewee: You mention there being problems despite the NGO's involvement. There may be an opportunity to explore if anything can be done to improve this. Being in international logistics our client may have expertise in moving large quantities of goods through international ports, though in this case it may be limited to airports. Would you like me to dive deeper into this area or should we explore some of the other potential opportunities?

(The interviewer could go in several different directions at this point.)

Firm: No, let's stop here. Based on the information you have, what would be your recommendation?

(The interviewer may want to end the interview or move to another part of it. Even if you feel you only scratched the surface, you need to make a recommendation. You should try to supplement your recommendation by proposing what the next steps might be.)

Interviewee: Based on the preliminary information thus far, I would recommend our client explore if there is an opportunity to combine its logistics expertise with the NGO's transportation-related work. There may be a second opportunity in communication or education. If none of these leads to the development of a suitable program, the client may need to consider looking for a different partner. However, it needs to realize that there may be only a limited number of NGOs capable of working on a global scope as they want to.

Firm: Now, assume you have got this far before you even started working on site. How would you structure your work once you get there?

Visit the Vault Consulting Career Channel at **www.vault.com/consulting** — with insider firm profiles, message boards, the Vault Consulting Job Board and more.

VAULT CAREER LIBRARY

95

(You need to outline a high-level workplan. If you can tie it into the structure you used during the interview, even better.)

Interviewee: Similar to my previously outlined structure, I see two distinct parts to this project. The first is looking for a way to further the partnership, and the second is to assess if this partnership is creating value for the client. I would work on the first part in a three-phase structure. In the first phase, I would confirm the client and the NGO's goals for this partnership, understand the NGO's work in depth, the client's core competencies based on its lines of business and then look for areas of overlap. In the second phase, I would concentrate on looking for projects the two organizations can work on in these areas. If any are found, the third phase would be assessing their suitability given the resources the client is willing to commit and its business objectives— for example, can the work of the project be duplicated, is the output going to contribute to the corporate image, and so on.

The second part of this project is, I think, our responsibility to the client to evaluate the partnership regardless of whether or not any suitable project is found. I would analyze why there was a lack of progress for so long, use the phase one work to assess future potential for this partnership and review what the other options are for the client. This could take place after the first part of our project or run in parallel as a second workstream.

Firm: I think that's suitable. Thank you.

Case analysis

This case is about assessing whether there is an opportunity to develop an existing partnership, and whether there is any value in continuing with it, given the business objectives of the client. The interviewer chose not to go into too much depth in analyzing individual options, but directed the discussion toward reaching an initial assessment, and formulated a structure for project planning. The interviewer could have handled this case in several ways. One would be to do a deep dive into a particular option, i.e., analyzing business fit, comparing resource (HR, financial) requirements with what the company was willing to commit, and so on. The interviewer could have also tried to challenge your creativity by asking you to identify several potential options for this partnership. A third option could have been to quickly guide you towards the conclusion that there was little scope for developing this partnership, and then asking you to work through the decision-making process of whether or not to dissolve it. In the version presented above, the end to the interview may seem a bit abrupt, but this could be an attempt to throw you off or to see how you summarize and close a discussion when you have very limited information.

 © 2008 Vault.com Inc.

Nonprofit Brand Case

Case question/background information provided

The board of a large, U.S.-based nonprofit organization has hired us to help them with a branding problem that the organization is currently having. They received some bad press because of financial mismanagement a few years ago, and while the guilty parties are no longer with the organization, the board feels that the brand is still tarnished—and they've also seen a decline in the amount of funds that the organization has raised in the last couple years. They've hired us to help turn that around. How would you structure this?

Additional information provided during questioning

• The client organization serves two main functions: 1) it raises millions of dollars through an extensive, countrywide umbrella organization, and 2) it divides up those funds (plus funds that it receives from some investments and from "program membership fees") amongst grassroots, nonpartisan, nonreligious community organizations serving the poor, children, the elderly and the disabled.

• The client organization has traditionally had a very recognizable brand, and still does. Brand awareness and recall is extraordinary throughout the country.

• (If the interviewee asks) The recent financial mismanagement heavily covered in the press was: the CEO of the organization was caught expensing lavish business trips (staying at the Four Seasons and such), as well as employing family members and paying them incredibly high salaries. This story was covered in national print and broadcast press. He resigned at the time of the story (as did his family members working at the organization), but the board feels that a lot of the damage lingers.

• Because the client is the board of the organization, and not senior management, the role of senior management—even their existence—is definitely in play.

• (A savvy interviewee might ask about the difference between having the board as the client and senior management as the client. If asked, the interviewer should say that it means that senior management's role/judgment is definitely being questioned and should be considered as part of the potential solution of the case.)

It may throw interviewees off, as the client is a nonprofit and not a standard for-profit corporation, which most cases are about. Still, many consulting firms do a significant amount of nonprofit work these days—many also are hired by large nonprofits in the same way they are by for-profits—so, it would not be surprising for a firm to give a case interview with a nonprofit setting. Furthermore, interviewees can apply the same case structuring and analysis techniques in the nonprofit setting that they would in a for-profit case.

That being said, this is a simple branding/revenue problem case. Because it is a marketing case, the four Ps and the three Cs are really the best structure to use to set the case up. Both are shown for the structuring part of the case, but the four Ps are utilized throughout, as they lead in best to the quantitative analysis needed to make a solid recommendation to the client.

Breakdown of solution

Interviewee: So, let me just make sure that I understand the case. The client is a not-for-profit organization, not a for-profit corporation. The board of directors has hired us to help them with their somewhat tarnished brand, and with a decline in donations?

Firm: Well, that's mostly right. They've seen a decline in their funds—which are not necessarily just donations. Let me explain a bit about our client. The client's organization serves two main functions: 1) it raises millions of dollars through an extensive, countrywide umbrella organization, and 2) it divides up those funds amongst grassroots, nonpartisan, nonreligious community organizations serving the poor, children, the elderly and the disabled. So, it's seen a decline in the funds that it has to divide up between its member organizations, but those funds come from four sources:

1) Donations from donors

2) Half the interest from the organization's investments

3) Fees from "membership dues" for the programs sponsored by the client organization

4) Promotional services fees, or fees that it collects from not-for-profits and for-profits that want to use the client's name/brand in its promotional material or products

Interviewee: Ah, interesting. So, the organization's revenue-generation model is more complicated than just donations from donors. That's good to know. Before I structure that case, can I get a better understanding of a couple of other things about the client and the case?

© 2008 Vault.com Inc.

Firm: Sure, go right ahead—ask away.

Interviewee: You mentioned that the client had been in the news lately—and not in a good way. Can I ask what that was about?

Firm: Sure. The recent financial mismanagement that was heavily covered in the press involved the CEO of the organization, who was found to be expensing lavish business trips (staying at the Four Seasons and such), as well as employing family members and paying them incredibly high salaries. This story was covered in national print and broadcast press. He resigned at the time of the story (as did his family members working at the organization), but the board feels that a lot of the damage still lingers.

Interviewee: Do we have a sense of how the client's brand is viewed?

Firm: Well, we can get further into that in the case, but for now, let's just say that organization has traditionally had a very recognizable brand, and still does. Brand awareness and recall is extraordinary throughout the country.

Interviewee: I just have one last question: You mentioned that we were hired by the board, not the new CEO. I've never worked for a board before—how is that different than working for the CEO of an organization?

Firm: That's a good question. Because the client is the board of the organization, and not senior management, the role of senior management—even their existence—is definitely in play, and should be considered when developing a solution to the case. So, are you ready to structure how you might approach this problem? Why don't you take a few minutes to sketch out your thoughts and approach.

(The interviewee's sketch is illustrated on page 100.)

Interviewee: Well, even though this is a nonprofit client, this still seems like a simple marketing problem to me, so I would use a simple marketing framework to approach the case. First, I would look at our product—the community service organizations that we fund. Maybe we're not funding the neediest of organizations, and that's hurting our brand and our revenue. Second, I would look at placement—maybe we're not in the neediest communities, or countries. Third, I would look at our promotion. I hope that we've started promoting our brand differently, or at least stepped up our brand promotion efforts, given the recent bad press that we've had. Last, I would look at our price. Now, that's a tricky one. I'm not sure what the price would be in this situation—maybe it's the fees that we charge our program members, or the fees we charge for promotional use of our brand, or maybe it's something with our donors?

Visit the Vault Consulting Career Channel at **www.vault.com/consulting** — with insider firm profiles, message boards, the Vault Consulting Job Board and more.

VAULT CAREER LIBRARY   99

(A summary of the structure of this approach follows.)

PRODUCT
- Has our product changed? Has our product portfolio changed?
- Does the product no longer suit market needs?
- What products are now out in the market?
- How do they compare to ours? Can we create new, customized products that can succeed in the market?

PRICE
- How is our product (donations, program fees and promotional activities fees) priced?
- Cost plus pricing? Market pricing?
- How does our product's price compare to that of our competition in the market?
- Can we change our price to succeed in the market?

PLACEMENT
- Is our product placed in the right markets?
- Are we global, national or local in our placement efforts? Are we in the neediest communities? Best donor markets?
- Are we placed in places accessible to donors?
- Event-based placement?
- Seasonal placement?
- Daily placement?

PROMOTION
- How are we marketing our product?
- Has our promotion changed recently? (It probably should have increased, given recent bad press.)
- Have our competitors' promotional activities changed recently? Has the level of promotional activity in the market changed?

Firm: That's great. You brought up a couple of interesting things that we discovered. In terms of product, we focus solely on the U.S., not international, which may have made us lose ground to some international nonprofit fundraising organizations.

Interviewee: Wow—so, globalization hits the nonprofit world as well!

Firm: Yes, it does. Second, we looked at our recent promotional spend, and that hadn't really increased since the bad press.

© 2008 Vault.com Inc.

Interviewee: That seems a little strange—wouldn't you want to step up good promotion and press when you've just had a bit of bad press?

Firm: Yes, that's what we thought, too. In all fairness, though, after a few conversations with the CEO, we found out that he froze all budgets because of the bad press. The bad press had to do with financial mismanagement, so he wanted to makes sure that there were no increases in any spending other than spending on the community service programs.

Interviewee: I could see that. It's probably still hurt the brand a bit.

Firm: Agreed. Now, turning to pricing, you had some interesting thoughts on that. Let's talk about pricing for a bit, specifically the pricing of donations. What do you think the price of donations is in a not-for-profit like this?

Interviewee: Is it the tiers that donors can give?

(The interviewer will likely let the interviewee guess a bit about this one before showing the exhibit and explaining how pricing works for the nonprofit donor organization client and its competitor.)

Firm: Well, that's a good guess, but other organizations have tiers, too, and our tiers are in line with the competition. Let me show you some data that we collected where we saw something very interesting.

Exhibit 1: The pricing of donation types

Client		City Competitor		Global Competitor	
Donations	$70 M	Donations	$50 M	Donations	$100 M
Investment Income	$5 M	Investment Income	$0 M	Investment Income	$50 M
Program Fees	$20 M	Program Fees	$0 M	Program Fees	$0 M
Promotional Services Fees	$5 M	Board Fees	$20 M	Promotional Services Fees	$0 M
Total Revenues	$100 M	Total Revenues	$70 M	Total Revenues	$150 M
Investor/ Donor Relations	$5 M	Investor/ Donor Relations	$0 M	Investor/ Donor Relations	$10 M
Administrative Expenses	$25	Administrative Expenses	$5 M	Administrative Expenses	$25 M
Selling/ Fundraising Expenses	$7 M	Selling/ Fundraising Expenses	$10 M	Selling/ Fundraising Expenses	$10 M
General Expenses	$8 M	General Expenses	$5 M	General Expenses	$10 M
Program Expenses	$65 M	Program Expenses	$50 M	Program Expenses	$95 M
Total Costs	$100 M	Total Costs	$ 70 M	Total Costs	$150 M

Visit the Vault Consulting Career Channel at **www.vault.com/consulting** — with insider firm profiles, message boards, the Vault Consulting Job Board and more.

VAULT CAREER LIBRARY   **101**

Firm: What does this exhibit tell you about the client relative to competitors?

Interviewee: Well, on the revenue side, I can see that we're not the biggest nonprofit donor organization out there—it looks like we're right in the middle based on revenue. But, it looks like we receive about the same amount—$50 million—in donations as does a city competitor, which is smaller than us. I know we're a national organization, so that's a bit surprising. I can also see that we're the only ones getting revenue from program fees and promotional services fees. Why is that?

Firm: Let's take each separately, and see what we can learn. First, the program fees are something the client has been doing since the beginning. It started charging each community service organization that received its funds a fee for the administration of fund, reporting, etc. It's basically a way to spread some of the client organization's overhead out to the community service organizations it raises funds for. How do you think that impacts the case?

Interviewee: Well, first, I imagine community service organizations like to receive funds from other donor organizations that don't charge them. Second, it may impact our brand out in the community, with grassroots community workers.

Firm: That's about right. Now, the promotional services fees are a newer revenue stream. When corporations started wanting to identify themselves with community service, we started charging them a fee to use our brand name in association with their community service and promotional fees. How do you think that has impacted the client's current problem?

Interviewee: Well, I'm not sure that it helps to have your brand associated with practically any corporation out there.

Firm: That's what we thought, too. Now, turning back to price. Looking at these abbreviated income statements, what do you think price is in this setting?

(If the interviewee doesn't see this, that's fine. But advanced interviewees—business school grads—should do their best to arrive at an answer.)

Interviewee: Well, if I look at the "Program Expenses" line item, I suppose that that's what actually was passed on to the community service programs, correct?

Firm: Yes, that's right. So, how much is that for each donor organization on Exhibit 1 for each donation dollar?

(This is a clear hint from the interviewer.)

© 2008 Vault.com Inc.

Interviewee: Well, for our client, for each donation dollar, it looks like only ($65 million/$70 million = .928) 93 cents goes to funding the community service organizations that it works with. As for the city competitor, first, what does "Board Fees" mean?

Firm: Well, that's an interesting question. We thought this organization was really interesting to benchmark because it does something very unique: it has its board pay for all of the organization's overhead so that every donor dollar goes to the grassroots community service organizations that it works with.

Interviewee: Interesting. So, for this organization, each donation dollar is a dollar in funds for the community organizations.

Firm: Right.

Interviewee: And for the global competitor, it looks like for each donation dollar, 95 cents gets passed on ($95 million/$100 million = .95). Wow, we're the most costly organization—more of every donor dollar given to us goes to pay our overhead than for our competitors.

Firm: That's right—and that's the price in this setting. So, given everything that we've discussed, what's your recommendation to the client?

Interviewee: Well, I would recommend three key changes going forward:

1) increase current promotional spend to help the brand tarnished by recent press coverage; the CEO was probably right to put a freeze on budget increases, but our brand now needs help to recover and regain our lost donations.

2) re-evaluate our promotional activities' revenue stream—the brand needs to be refurbished, and lending it out to corporations for fees that comprise so little of our revenue may be detracting more than it's adding.

3) change our cost structure so that we can bring our "pricing" in line with that of the competition—donors are finding more value elsewhere, and we're losing revenue by not staying competitive.

(It's key here that the interviewee remember his client is the board, not the CEO.)

Firm: Great. I think that sums it up nicely.

Norwegian Widgets Case

Your client is a Norwegian firm that produces widgets and ships them to business and residential customers throughout Europe. In a recent review of its financial metrics, the CFO noticed that the products transportation cost has been steadily increasing as a percentage of costs over the past two years and is eating into profitability.

You have been asked to determine the reason for this and to recommend what should be done to restore the lost profitability margin.

(You have been given a situation where a very specific cost bucket is being analyzed. This gives you a narrow range to focus on, but may indicate that the interviewer is expecting you to go into some detail as you move through the case. You will also need to decide if there is information relevant to specific details, such as the client being in Norway [the interviewer will not expect you to have specific knowledge of Norway beforehand]. Start with giving a structure to your planned analysis.)

Interviewee: The CFO is concerned about a specific cost bucket that is leading to declining profitability. I would like to structure my analysis by first understanding a little bit more about the client's business and if there are specific location characteristics that are important to its situation. Next, I would like to delve into the drivers of the transportation costs and determine if any have changed over the past two years. Here again I would like to examine if being in Norway creates some specific location characteristics that are important to consider. This should lead me to understand the reasons for the rise in costs in this area. The next step will be to see if we can develop solutions to these causes. If we hit a roadblock here, then I would like to look for alternatives that can be developed to reverse the cost increase. If again we hit a roadblock at this point, another option to restore profitability might be to look for other cost buckets that can be controlled, or examine if there is an opportunity to increase the volume of goods produced to increase overall profitability.

(It is good to introduce the last option to indicate you are able to think about the client beyond just its current focus and will have an avenue to explore in case the main one does not result in any solutions. You should also mention reviewing any location-specific characteristics because at this time you do not know if they will play a role or not.)

Firm: I think that's OK.

(When outlining an analysis structure, you should be prepared for an interviewer to ask you to jump straight to an intermediate step that you outlined.)

Interviewee: As outlined, I would like to first understand more about the client. Can you tell me about the firm?

Firm: What would you like to know?

(It's OK to start with a very open question to see what the interviewer provides you. But if the interviewer indicates you need to be more specific, try to be more focused in your questions going forward.)

Interviewee: Could you tell me about the widgets the client produces? What are they? I am asking because I am wondering if they require specialized transportation arrangements.

Firm: For this case, assume the widgets are just some plastic objects. They do not need any special transport arrangements. They are sold at a fixed price to customers—as part of its promotional campaign the company decided not to charge the shipping and handling costs to customers.

Interviewee: Could you tell me about the current transportation arrangements the client uses for these widgets? For example, does the company transport the widgets themselves?

Firm: No, the company does not have any kind of infrastructure to transport things across Europe. It only manufactures them.

(The interviewer has only answered part of the question. He or she has not answered how the transportation is actually done. He may have simply forgotten or he could be checking to see if you paid attention to what he said and realized that your question was not fully answered. Be alert and don't be afraid to repeat your question.)

Interviewee: So if the client does not transport the widgets itself, how is it currently doing it?

Firm: Well, the widgets are quite simple, and it's just a question of picking them up from the factory and dropping them off at another place. The firm currently has a contract with a transport company, which does the door-to-door delivery and handles everything in between, from customs to insurance to everything else for all of the client's widgets.

Interviewee: So would it be correct to say then that the transportation cost being analyzed is entirely from this contract, or is there any other aspect?

Firm: That's correct. Transportation costs for this widget are basically a bill paid to the transport company at the end of each quarter.

(You've identified where the costs are coming from. It's time to move to the next step to understand what the drivers are.)

Visit the Vault Consulting Career Channel at **www.vault.com/consulting** — with insider firm profiles, message boards, the Vault Consulting Job Board and more.

VAULT CAREER LIBRARY   **105**

Interviewee: Now that we know that the cost is based entirely on the agreement between our client and the transport company, I'd like to move on to the next part of my analysis and dive into this.

(It might be a good idea to periodically refer back to your original analysis structure as you go through the interview to show the interviewer you are using it and have not forgotten about it.)

Firm: Sure.

Interviewee: Do we know any details about the contract? For example, are the charges based on a fixed price per unit for particular destinations? Is there a minimum volume required? Or any other details?

Firm: The contract has two pricing schemes in it. The first is for delivery to business customers and the second is for delivery to residential customers. Business customers always receive shipments by 9 a.m. and the client is charged a fixed price per unit. This price varies from city to city of course. When the unit is delivered to an individual residential consumer, then the rate charged is much more variable and depends on the specifications of the delivery, such as timing, number of repeat visits required, whether or not a consignee signature is required and so on. There are no minimum volume requirements needed from the client.

Interviewee: Has there been any major increase in the transport company's charges in the past two years that are not volume-related?

Firm: There have been some changes for inflation, fuel surcharge adjustments and so on, but nothing at the per unit level that is drastic enough or of a sustained nature to cause the profit reduction seen over the last two years.

Interviewee: Are there any volume discounts offered to the client?

Firm: Yes, these are negotiated annually for the two types of delivery locations. The CFO and procurement teams are satisfied that these are fair.

Interviewee: Has the client ever compared the transportation rates offered by other companies and whether they are competitive with what's offered by the current transport company?

Firm: Yes, this is part of the annual review done by the procurement department, which is satisfied that no other transport companies are offering a more competitive rate.

Interviewee: Has the client ever considered the costs and long-run benefits of developing its own transportation network so that it doesn't need to go through a partner?

© 2008 Vault.com Inc.

Firm: Yes, this was found to be highly impractical and very expensive to set up.

(The last few questions have not provided you any directions in which to proceed. They are nonetheless valuable to help you eliminate options as well as show the interviewer that you are thinking of several different possibilities. But you do not want to appear as if you are "shooting in the dark." You need to take stock of what information you have and whether you have overlooked anything; frame this positively.)

Interviewee: I'd like to take a minute to review the information to see if I have overlooked anything or if I should move on to another area of analysis.

Firm: Sure.

(You should not take more than about a minute here to review your information and decide how to proceed. You want to make sure you have not left anything unexplored regarding the transportation contract before moving on. In this case, we have not yet looked at why there is a different pricing scheme for business and residential customers and what impact this may have, if any.)

Interviewee: I'd like to better understand the pricing used in the contract to know why deliveries to business and residential customers follow a different pricing scheme.

Firm: It's been like this from the start. The client has always had far more volume going to business customers and negotiated a flat rate for them for each city. When the contract was first developed, such a flat rate for residential customers would have been a lot more expensive on average since the volume was low.

Interviewee: Is this distribution of business and residential customers the same even today?

Firm: Even today there are far more business customers than residential ones, but the rate of new customers being added is different. Residential customers are being added at a faster rate in certain countries.

(You have found that the client's customer base is changing and this directly affects the two components of its transportation costs. You definitely want to explore this further. Try to talk the interviewer through the thinking behind looking into this difference.)

Interviewee: If residential customers are increasing at a faster rate, they are becoming an increasing percentage of our client's customers; thus a larger percentage of deliveries are on the variable pricing scheme and not the flat rate. I'd like to look at what affect this has had on the overall costs. Has the average cost of delivery to a residential customer been rising?   .

Firm: Yes, the average cost has been rising by about 1 percent per year.

Interviewee: And for business customers?

Firm: The average cost for business customer has been declining marginally as they gain greater volume.

Interviewee: How does this increase for residential customers compare to changes in other cost areas for manufacturing the product?

Firm: Other cost areas have been rising 0.3 percent to 0.5 percent annually.

(Do some quick mental math here. If one cost bucket is increasing at a faster rate than the others, it is becoming a higher percentage of the total costs. Now pair this with the fact that the customer group this change applies to is becoming a larger part of the overall customer base. Once you have thought this through, present your initial assessment.)

Interviewee: It seems that the transportation costs are rising faster than other costs for residential customers. These customers are also becoming a larger part of the customer base. This explains why they now constitute a larger part of the overall costs. I would need to examine actual figures, but my assumption would be that the increase in costs to residential customers is offsetting the gains from cost reductions to business customers and therefore eating into overall profitability.

Firm: Do you think we should drop the residential customers to focus only on the more profitable customers?

Interviewee: Based on the information I have, I would not recommend ignoring residential customers at this time. Rather, my initial recommendation is to re-evaluate the pricing scheme used for transporting the widgets to residential customers. I am currently assuming that the trend of residential customers increasing at a faster rate is going to continue, so we can expect the volume of shipments to residential customers to increase. This assumption will, of course, need to be verified. The client should evaluate if a fixed price contract will provide a better scale similar to the effect seen with business customers. We would also need to understand at what number of units shipped a flat pricing scheme becomes a more cost-effective proposition. If this number is lower than what we are currently shipping then the client should consider switching at the earliest possible time.

Firm: I think that is a reasonable suggestion but it is dependent on the transport partner also agreeing to re-evaluate the pricing contract, as well as a flat rate that is low enough to make this change valuable. What would you suggest as a backup in case they are not willing to do this?

© 2008 Vault.com Inc.

Interviewee: I would proceed to the final step I had mentioned in my outline, which is to see if there are other cost buckets that can be reduced to make up for this increase. I would simultaneously consider the feasibility of a fresh tender to transportation companies, this time asking for proposals with a flat rate for both kinds of customers. Although we have previously not found them competitive, they may become so with a different pricing scheme.

Firm: Thank you.

Case analysis

This is a case about delving into the various components of the transportation costs for a product to determine what is driving it up. This is combined with uncovering different pricing schemes for different customer segments. An error in this case would have been to assume everyone was on the same pricing scheme. In general, it is almost always important to look for differences in customer segments, whether from a profitability or a cost point of view. It is also important to distinguish between driving down overall transportation costs and controlling them as a percentage of the overall costs.

The case could have gone down a different path where there was no opportunity to control the transportation costs for either customer segment. You would then need to look at whether any other costs can be brought down to compensate. This can change the focus of the case and test your broader knowledge of different cost buckets and what their influencers might be. Recognizing this possibility early on, when setting up your analysis structure, will help prevent you from forgetting to consider it when you are wrapped up in a different area.

Online Gambling Case

A large, global gambling company is the client. The executives have noticed the explosion in the growth of online gambling and have hired us to help them evaluate and create their market entry strategy. How would you structure that?

Additional information provided during questioning

• The client is a large gambling company. They have operations in 40 countries worldwide and are considering the online gambling market worldwide in this endeavor. The firm is also a U.S.-based company.

Visit the Vault Consulting Career Channel at www.vault.com/consulting — with insider firm profiles, message boards, the Vault Consulting Job Board and more.

VAULT CAREER LIBRARY   **109**

• The client runs several types of gaming operations. First, it facilitates lotteries for governments globally—it develops the games, runs the transaction network and handles the operations of the lottery. Second, it runs a chain of casinos with operations in both the U.S. and overseas. Third, it owns and operates slot machines that are placed in off-gaming sites; this business is purely international, but growing.

• The online gambling market has experienced tremendous growth in the last decade. In 1996, bets for the online gambling industry totaled approximately $17 million. In 2007, the online gambling industry is expected to total $18 billion.

Suggested high-level overview of solution

The framework that an interviewee should be aware of is the decision tree for market entry (see framework included). Once the interviewee has shown that he or she can structure the case well, he or she should just use the data provided effectively to answer the secondary case questions and summarize the findings at the end.

Numbers do not drive this case. There's a quick quantitative question in the beginning of the case to get the interviewee thinking. There is also a short quantitative exercise thrown in at the end to help the interviewer test the interviewee's comfort with numbers, but it does not drive the case answer. Also, the quantitative exercise is literally tacked on to the end of the case—it may surprise the interviewee that it is even there. This is also meant to test the interviewee to see how he or she reacts to surprises in the case format.

Breakdown of solution (including quantitative analyses and qualitative evaluations)

Interviewee: I'd like to make sure that I understand the case.

Firm: Go right ahead. What questions do you have for me?

Interviewee: Our client is a large, global but U.S.-based gambling company, and is interested in entering the online gambling market. We've been hired to help determine its strategy for doing that. I'm assuming that it doesn't currently have any online gambling operations. Is that correct?

Firm: Yes, that's correct. The client is a large gambling company. It has operations in 40 countries worldwide and is considering the online gambling market worldwide in this endeavor. The client runs several types of gaming operations. First, it facilitates lotteries for governments globally—it develops the games, runs the transaction network and handles the operations of the lottery. Second, it runs a chain of casinos with operations in both the U.S. and overseas. Third, it owns and operates

© 2008 Vault.com Inc.

slot machines that are placed in off-gaming sites; this business is purely an international business, but a growing one. And no, currently, it has no online gambling operations, but it has now hired us to help with how to get into that market.

Interviewee: OK, and can I assume that it's a pretty attractive market to get into, or should I evaluate that, too?

Firm: No, no need to evaluate that, too. Actually, before we even get into the case, let's talk about what we know about the market first.

(This is not a "standard" case flow, but an interviewee should be prepared for anything to happen here. A case interviewer might want to discuss case data before getting into the structured case—and he or she also might be testing an interviewee's abilities to "roll with the punches." So, a good interviewee will be able to shift gears and participate in whatever discussion an interviewer initiates.)

Interviewee: Okay, that'd be great. What do we know about the market so far?

Firm: We've done some quick due diligence already, and it's a pretty attractive, fast-growing market. The online gambling market has experienced tremendous growth in the last 10 years. In 1996, bets for the online gambling industry totaled approximately $17 million. This year, the online gambling industry is expected to total $18 billion. Just quickly, what kind of a growth rate are we talking about there?

(Here, the interviewer is testing an interviewee's quant skills)

Interviewee: Well, if it started at $17 million, and it's now over $17 billion, that's a grow rate of over 1,000 percent.

(Here, the interviewee has used 17 billion, instead of 18 billion, in order to make the math easier, which in this case is probably fine. But interviewees should prepare themselves to do more exact math in case an interviewer is a stickler for the numbers!)

Firm: Yes, that's right. What do you think about that growth?

(Here, the interviewer is trying to test the interviewee's business judgment/intuition.)

Interviewee: In general, it looks great, but growth like that really isn't sustainable. I imagine that the online gambling industry is pretty new and in its startup phase and that industry growth rates will decline as the industry matures. I also wonder how accurate the industry metrics are in such a new industry/market. Oftentimes, in a new industry, the metrics for that industry aren't that reliable, as standard measures and reporting mechanisms haven't become stable.

Firm: That's great—and that's right. The sheer industry sizing numbers that we got from third-party research helped us understand a bit about this new mar-

Visit the Vault Consulting Career Channel at **www.vault.com/consulting** — with insider firm profiles, message boards, the Vault Consulting Job Board and more.

VAULT CAREER LIBRARY   **111**

ket. But we wanted to know more about it. Let me show you some other data that we collected. What does that tell you about the online gambling industry?

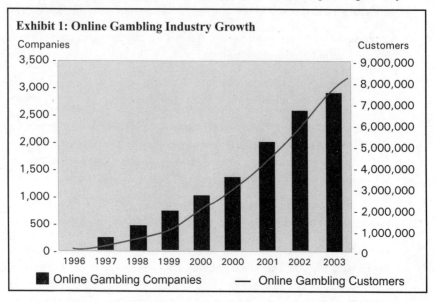

Exhibit 1: Online Gambling Industry Growth

Interviewee: Well, it tells me a couple of things. First, it reinforces the fact that this market is still in startup and high-growth mode. Second, it shows me that the industry is highly fragmented—the number of online gambling companies continues to grow rapidly. My guess is that there aren't real barriers to entry—any company can come in and customers aren't necessarily loyal to any single company, product or brand. Third, it looks like online gambling is somewhat recession-proof. I mean, the Internet boom kind of went bust in 2000/2001, and yet the number of online gambling companies and customers continued to grow in this online market. Finally, it looks like there's still room for the industry to grow—new customers are still coming; so, this market will likely get bigger.

(If the interviewee gets two or three of these observations, he or she has done a good job. In fact, he or she should make at least two observations. If not, the interviewer should press the interviewee to come up with more.)

Firm: That's great. Now that you know a bit more about the industry, you're where we and the client were at the beginning of this case. How would you structure how to enter this market?

Interviewee: May I have a few minutes to collect my thoughts?

Firm: Of course. Take your time.

(Few minutes go by ...)

© 2008 Vault.com Inc.

Interviewee: Well, with any new market entry, I think a firm has three options: 1) create a new business organically from existing lines of business and divisions, 2) get into that market by making a significant acquisition already in that market—or a series of acquisitions in that market, or 3) create that business by a mix of both organic growth and acquisitions.

(The three options are illustrated in the table below.)

Marketing Entry Strategy	• Create online gambling business organically.
	    • Create an online gambling division within the company using its existing resources, products, services or brands.
	
	• Create online gambling business through acquisition.
	    • Buy an online gambling company (or companies) to enter the market through an existing player with existing brands and customers.
	
	• Create an online gambling business through a mixture of organic growth and acquisition.
	    • Make targeted, small acquisitions that will quickly mesh with existing businesses to create online gambling business.

Firm: That's right. Now, knowing what you know about this client and this market, which would you suggest this client do?

(This is the key question for this case. Because there is little data that would drive an answer here, it doesn't matter so much which option an interviewee chooses—but he or she should make a recommendation with some data supporting it. The following is an example of an answer for each.)

Marketing Entry Strategy	• Create online gambling business organically.
	    • Use the consumer-focused divisions of the company and create online divisions that mirror existing consumer brands. For example, the client could create slot machine games online that mirror their existing slot machines in overseas markets.
	
	• Create online gambling business through acquisition.
	    • There are so many online gambling companies out there already; it might be easier to buy small companies in all of the geographic markets that the client wants to exist in. That would ensure quick market entry.
	
	• Create an online gambling business through a mixture of organic growth and acquisition.
	    • The client could make targeted acquisitions in markets where its existing consumer-focused businesses are not that developed.
	
	    • The client could grow its existing consumer-focused businesses in markets where its brands might translate easily online.

Visit the Vault Consulting Career Channel at www.vault.com/consulting — with insider firm profiles, message boards, the Vault Consulting Job Board and more.

VAULT CAREER LIBRARY   **113**

Interviewee: If the client has hired us, my guess is that it's pretty invested in entering this market. But it sounds like it also wants to do it in a low-risk fashion—if it's paying us to evaluate the market and create a strategy, it probably doesn't want to take huge risks. Because the market is still so fragmented—thousands of companies—it doesn't seem like there's one significant acquisition that the client could make to enter the market in a big way. But because there are so many companies out there, I bet it could pick up some acquisitions in key markets where the client might not have significant current assets that it can leverage. So, I would recommend a mix strategy: enter the online gambling market organically where the client has significant consumer-focused business that it can use as springboards to the online world and make select acquisitions of online gambling companies in geographic markets where it still needs some help.

Firm: That's great. And it's pretty close to what we actually recommended.

Interviewee: Great.

Firm: But this case actually led to another case for the firm. The client ended up hiring us to evaluate an acquisition target in the Japanese market, where it didn't have many current lines of business. The client wanted to buy this existing company because it thought that its product development capabilities would help bring more products to market, and faster. In fact, the client is hoping that this new company will allow it to bring an average of three new products to the Japanese market each year. We've done a bit of research to determine its R&D processes, which are summarized in the following.

Exhibit 2: Game Development Cycle

New Product Development Stage	Developer's Roundtable	R&D Board Screen	Finance Screen	Marketing Screen 1	Marketing Screen 2
Amount of Time for Stage of Development	6 months	3 months	6 months	6 months	3 months
% of Products Passing Stage	80%	60%	50%	50%	50%

© 2008 Vault.com Inc.

The company currently has about 100 products each year enter at the "Developer's Roundtable" stage. Given this data, do you think that the client should make this acquisition?

Interviewee: Well, let me make sure that I understand this data first. These are the five stages of the development with the time it takes at each stage, and new games must pass these five screens before being brought to market?

Firm: That's right. So, should the client acquire this company?

Interviewee: Well, if the client has 100 products enter at the Developer's Roundtable, and only 80 percent make it through that, then it has 80 products at the R&D board screen. If only 60 percent of the 80 make it beyond there, then only 48 enter the finance screen. From there, only 50 percent—or 24—make it to the next screen, which halves the number of products again to 12 and again on the last screen to six. So, at the end of the development process, which takes two years exactly, the client has six new products ready to take to market. If you average that out over the two years—that means this company can bring an average of three new products to market each year, which is what the client wants for the Japanese market. So, yes, if all else about the company is what the client is looking for, then yes, they should make the acquisition.

Firm: That's great. That's what we recommended, too.

Organic Fast-Food Case

Please read the following case carefully and answer the three questions. You may use the calculator, paper and pen made available to you. After 20 minutes, you will walk through your solutions with the consultant.

Situation

A small organic fast-food chain, Different Taste, with over three stores in Drywell, has been financially successful for the past couple of years and has decided to expand into the neighboring city of Ashland. The imperative for moving out to Ashland is the lack of suitable store locations in Drywell that will generate the same amount of traffic for future stores to be financially viable.

Background information

Unlike a typical food chain, it is imperative for the business development director, Jane, to ensure that there will be sufficient demand sustaining the store, and for future expansion. She has already determined that there are no similar competitors in

Ashland. The targeted location in Ashland will attract customers of similar socioe-conomic demographics as Drywell's stores. However, this is the first time her business development team is considering opening up a store outside of Drywell, a city of three million. Therefore, they are gathering a lot of data to ensure that they will be making the right decision.

Success of Drywell's stores

To make a calculated decision to open a store in Ashland, Jane needs to evaluate why the store's current expansion into Drywell has been so successful.

The organic fast-food chain has the same menu as a typical hamburger joint, but all of the food is made from organic cheese, meat, buns and vegetables, etc. The oil used to prepare the food is also lowfat and organic. The drinks are mostly healthy, consisting of organic fruit juice, organic milk and mineral water. Given the high cost of raw materials, there is a price premium for the products sold, but customers are willing to pay the 15 to 25 percent premium over other fast-food chains for the healthy, tasty and convenient food. All of the three stores are situated in the downtown shopping areas in the central part of the city. The in-store environments are brightly lit and clean, with comfortable seats. The management deliberately chose not to have any Internet access in order to attract patrons who are only having meals.

Six months ago, they conducted a survey of their customer base, and as expected, the survey found that the customers are mostly well educated and stem from the higher income brackets. Surprisingly, families with young children tend to patronize the stores during mealtime on weekdays. Different Taste is perceived as a healthy alternative to a family dinner, and the children actually find the food "fun" to eat. The customers come from the surrounding suburbs, in addition to the suburb the store is located in. Based on the survey data, and evaluating the location of the proposed store in Ashland, Jane's team is confident that the most likely number of customers each month is 14,500.

Revenue of current stores

Jane has gathered data for the past 12 months from the three stores (see Exhibit 1 on page 118), and analyzed it thoroughly. Revenue is driven by spending per customer and number of customers who purchased from the stores. Jane has further details in terms of the percentage of take-away sales and dining in. Take-away is almost 60 percent of total revenue, but lower than the 70 to 75 percent of other fast-food chains.

© 2008 Vault.com Inc.

Costs of running the current stores

The major cost components are the raw materials for food and drink, rental costs and labor. Different Taste has not reached economies of scale to lease or purchase its store locations. The cost of the food is reflected as a percentage of the revenue sales, as it is able to achieve some economies of scale in purchasing. For Drywell's stores, the average cost of the raw materials is 31 percent of the revenue. However, due to the targeted city being an hour away from its three stores, Jane's team estimates that the raw materials will cost an additional 2 percent of the revenue sold. This is due to additional transportation costs and lack of economies of scale, rather than the current average 31 percent of the three stores.

The labor cost (see Exhibit 2 on page 118) comes from the number of workers hired in proportion to the number of customers. In terms of rental cost (see Exhibit 3 on page 119), there is a strong correlation to the number of customers, as better located stores are situated in high-traffic areas.

The targeted gross profit is expected to be 30 percent for a new store to be profitable, due to corporate overhead cost, cost of capital and other miscellaneous items.

Should Different Taste expand into Ashland?

Jane is aware of the importance of the decision, as it is the first time Different Taste has decided to expand outside its area of comfort. If the targeted gross profit is below 30 percent, it is unlikely that the CEO will agree to the expansion for the time being. Jane needs to quickly determine whether it is feasible, before going into more detail, to recheck all the assumptions. She needs to make a financially driven recommendation about whether Different Taste should expand into Ashland.

Exhibit 1: Spend per customer and number of customers

Average spend per customer per store in Drywell in past 12 months ($)

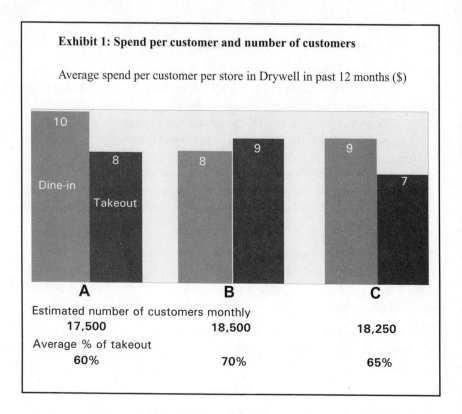

	A	B	C
Estimated number of customers monthly	17,500	18,500	18,250
Average % of takeout	60%	70%	65%

Exhibit 2: Labor cost

Average number of workers in each store in Drywell

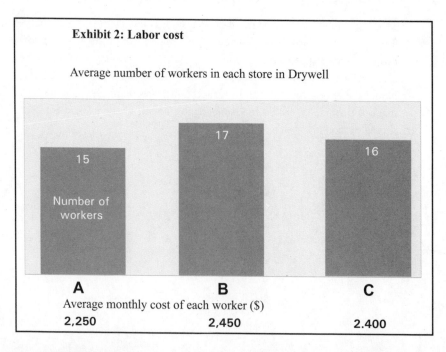

	A	B	C
Average monthly cost of each worker ($)	2,250	2,450	2,400

© 2008 Vault.com Inc.

Exhibit 3: Rental Cost

Average rental cost* per month for each store in Drywell

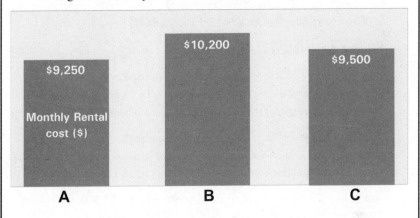

Note: * Rental costs include average utilities, etc.

Exhibit 4: Projected data for new store in Ashland

Revenue Items

Estimated number of customers	14,500
Average spend per customer per store	To be estimated from average of Drywell's stores
Percentage of take-away customers	65%

Cost Items

Monthly Rental Cost*	$8,500
Number of workers needed	To be estimated from projected number of customers in Ashland
Average monthly cost for each worker ($)	65%
Cost of raw material	33% of revenue

Note: * Rental cost include average utilities, etc.
Source: Estimated from Jane's business development team

Questions (and answers)

Will the new store in Ashland achieve at least a 30 percent gross profit given the estimated collected data? You must use the average data for the three stores to do any estimation for the new store economies.

Estimated monthly revenue from Ashland's store

Estimate the per customer spend for take-away and dine in.
Average customer spending for dine in for Drywell's stores = $(10+8+9)/3 = $9.
Average customer spending for take-away for Drywell's stores = $ (8+9+7)/3 = $8.

We will assume that the average customer spending for the Ashland store will be the same as Drywell's stores, as the targeted location in Ashland will attract customers of similar socioeconomic demographics as Drywell's stores.

Total takeout customer revenue = $14,500*65%*$8 = $75,400.
Total dine in customer revenue = $14,500*35%*$9 = $45,675.

Total estimated revenue from Ashland's store = $121,705.

Estimated monthly costs from running store in Ashland

Determine the number of workers needed for the store based on number of customers.

Average number of customers for stores in Drywell = $(17,500+18,500+18,250)/3 = $17,666
Average number of workers for stores in Drywell = (15+16+17)/3 = 16.
Average number of customers per worker in Drywell = 17,666/16 = 1,104.
Estimated number of worker needed for Ashland's store based on Drywell's stores = 14,500/1104 = 13.1 (14) (round up to obtain number of workers).

Estimated cost of running the store in Ashland

Labor cost = 14*$2,200 = $31,500.
Monthly rental cost (which includes average utilities spent) = $8,500 (estimated and given).
Food cost = (31+2) % of revenue = 33% * $121,705 = $39,995.
Total monthly cost of running store in Ashland = $79,995.

Determine gross profit of Ashland's stores

Gross Profit = $121,705 - $79,955 = $41,120.
Gross Profit percentage of revenue = $41,120/$121,705 = 34 percent.

Should Jane recommend that Different Taste enter Ashland, assuming the data available is accurate after checking?

From initial estimation, Different Taste will be able to achieve at least a 30 percent gross profit if it chooses to enter Ashland. Therefore, Jane should recommend that Different Taste expand into Ashland.

The profit margin of 4 percent above the target does suggest that Jane can be confident that if the number of customers hovers around 10 to 15 percent of the estimated 14,500 customers, the store in Ashland will definitely be able to hit its 30 percent gross profit target.

Regardless of the answer to two and assuming that Different Taste chooses to enter Ashland, how should the company go about doing so to ensure its success?

A. Ensuring the quality of estimated data

> 1.Ensure that more tangible data sources, such as monthly rent and cost of workers, have been checked to ensure accuracy.

> 2.Check that the location of the store will be able to generate the estimated number of customers from the correct socioeconomic demographic profile to drive the same amount of customer spending in Drywell.

B. Ensure the quality of the food, service and environment

> 3. In terms of raw materials, Different Taste will have to ensure that the quality remains consistent with the Drywell stores. Different Taste can do so by either sourcing from the current supplier, or from local suppliers who can guarantee the same freshness and quality.

> 4. The interior of the store must be of the same quality as the Drywell stores.

> 5. The staff must be as well trained and service-oriented as the Drywell stores.

C. Monitor the first few months closely to ensure store is customer-centric and economically viable.

> 6. Corporate HQ should observe the customers' behavior at the Ashland store, and modify food offerings and service levels accordingly. Even though it is unlikely that the customers in Ashland will differ significantly from Drywell, it is still important to ensure the store in Ashland remains customer-centric, in order to continue to drive customers into the store.

> 7. The Ashland financials should be monitored closely to ensure that the 30 percent gross profit is achieved. The aim is to achieve 30 percent gross profit as early as possible, ideally within the first two months.

Visit the Vault Consulting Career Channel at **www.vault.com/consulting** — with insider firm profiles, message boards, the Vault Consulting Job Board and more.

VAULT CAREER LIBRARY   **121**

Outsourcing Commercial Debt Collection Case

Your client is a North American financial institution specializing in third party B2C debt collection. It has had steady growth, with profit margins on par with the industry average. Seeing all the news surrounding IT offshore outsourcing, it is wondering if it can use the outsourcing business model to reduce its operational costs. It wants you help think this through.

One question it has is whether or not it should consider the offshore outsourcing business model. What should it consider outsourcing, if anything at all?

(This case is about assessing if the outsourcing business model can be applied to your client, with the specific goal of reducing operational costs. You need to understand the industry it operates in [which you may not be familiar with] and what outsourcing is all about [which you probably do understand and know a little bit about]. Start by exploring the industry.)

Interviewee: I understand the outsourcing business model, but am not familiar with the debt collection industry. Could you begin by briefly giving me some information about it so I can understand how our client fits in?

Firm: The debt collection industry is linked to accounts receivables management. To simplify a little, companies will often sell services and products to their customers on credit—which may initially be reflected in the accounts receivables section of their balance sheet—but eventually they have to collect this money. A percentage of it will be uncollectible for various reasons. In the case of B2B, perhaps the customer has become insolvent. The more common case is B2C—where, for example, perhaps the customer has simply left town, leaving behind an unpaid bill. In such cases, the company can write off the debt as a loss, or it can "sell" it to debt collectors. For example, if a company is owed $10, it will sell the "right to collect" the $10 to another company for say $2. This way it receives 20 percent of the money it's owed rather than 0 percent. The debt collector will try to collect the debt and may collect, say, $5 for debt it paid $2 for, thus making a profit on it. If it cannot collect any of it, it will either try to resell it to another debt collector or will write it off.

(You now know a little bit about the industry your client is in. You should already be familiar with the basics of the outsourcing business model. Remember, here you are dealing with offshore outsourcing and not just outsourcing [i.e., sending work halfway across the world rather than into the next town]. If you are not clear about outsourcing, you should ask the interviewer about it as well. Once you are comfortable with both topics, proceed by outlining a framework for your analysis.)

© 2008 Vault.com Inc.

Interviewee: I would like to use the following structure to analyze this situation. I need to fully understand the major steps our client goes through from the time it purchases the B2C debt to the time it either collects or decides to sell or write it off. This will help me better understand our client's business process. Next, I'd like to assess, from a purely operational view, if one or more of these steps is appropriate for outsourcing. If there are any, I'd like to see what would be the effect/reduction on operational costs if the client did outsource that step, and what is required to implement the outsourcing. I'd also like to check the feasibility of putting quality and monitoring checks in place to ensure that the client does not suffer in this respect, due to losing direct control over part of its business.

(The last part, a nice extra, shows the interviewer you can really put yourself in your clients' shoes to think about what they will be worried about beyond just the basics.)

Firm: I think that's appropriate. Where would you like to start?

Interviewee: First I need to understand the steps that take place between purchasing debt, and being able to collect it or deciding to write it off. Can you describe this process for me?

(The interviewer has likely given you some paper and a pen, or you have brought these with you. You should note down the steps as the interviewer outlines them, since it will be the focus of your analysis going forward and you do not want to forget any of the steps in the process. If you are a visually-driven person you should feel comfortable with sketching out diagrams with arrows or boxes, or whatever else works for you.)

Firm: At a high level, the process has three or four major steps. The client will purchase the debt and assign it to one of its staff, called a "debt collection agent." This is usually one of a large pool of people operating in a call center-type environment. This person will attempt, over several days, to locate the customer who owes the debt. If he does locate the person, he will try to contact him or her to collect payment. If the person is not willing to pay the money owed, a decision is made on whether or not to take legal action to try to force the person to pay. If a positive decision is made, then legal proceedings may be initiated. But more often than not, the decision will be negative, because the cost of legal proceedings will far exceed the value that may be collected, and the debt will be deemed uncollectible and either written off or an attempt made to sell to another company at a lower price. All of this operates within fairly strict legal frameworks of what a debt collection company can and cannot do to find a person, extract payment and so on.

(As outlined in your structure, you want to check if any of these steps would be appropriate for offshore outsourcing. The major advantage of offshore outsourcing is converting labor costs from fixed to variable and at a lower rate than could be achieved onshore [i.e., at the place the company is currently located]. In this case the interviewer has practically identified a potential opportunity for you by describing one of the steps as involving large number of people in a call center environment. You want to talk the interviewer through the thinking that makes you focus on this step rather than the others—this will also help you avoid making the mistake of simply jumping to the obvious candidat.).

Interviewee: Considering the major steps in this process, my assumption is that purchasing the debt is not a highly labor intensive process and depends on periodic contractual negotiations with companies looking to sell their debt.

Firm: Yes, that's mostly the case.

Interviewee: The next step that is carried out by debt collection agents appears to be more labor intensive, given that it is in a call center environment, and there may be an opportunity here. The third step, considering legal options, may also be time consuming, but I assume it will be more specialized work—again given that it would require familiarity with the relevant laws and so on, and thus may not be the best candidate for outsourcing. If you agree with my assumptions, as an early hypothesis, I would like to dig deeper into the second step and focus on the work done by the debt collection agents. If this does not develop into an opportunity then I may come back to the other two areas and examine them further.

(By identifying your assumptions and describing your line of reasoning, you show the interviewer you are not simply making guesses in the dark. Even if there is an error in your reasoning chain, the interviewer can correct it rather than the entire conclusion. This "thinking out loud" process is highly encouraged in case interviews and is something you should practice since it is not what people normally do. You also want to add the last line to leave yourself the option to return to this point in the analysis if the current branch does not develop as expected.)

Firm: I think those are reasonable assumptions, let's proceed by digging deeper into the debt collection agent's work.

Interviewee: I'd like to look at this from two points of view. The first is from a financial perspective. I would like to explore the cost of outsourcing, whether or not it would contribute to the business goal of reduced operational cost, and by how much. The second is from an operational point of view, looking at

© 2008 Vault.com Inc.

what would be involved in executing an outsourcing of this part of the work off-shore.

Firm: Sure, let's start with the financial perspective. Assume the client would find a partner in India, Malaysia or a similar place, and would not have to establish its own offices, do recruitment or basic training, and that other basic setup costs will be largely one-time expenses. How would you look at the second part of the financial decision to see if this is worth doing or not?

Interviewee: I would look at this in the context of the financial goals of the initiative, which were to reduce operating costs. What portion of our operating costs are the debt collection agents' and the overhead associated with them?

Firm: They comprise about 50 to 60 percent of the operating costs excluding one-off special items.

Interviewee: And do we have any estimates for what percentage an offshore labor cost pool would be?

Firm: We don't have any estimates right now. What would you examine to do a back-of-the-napkin style calculation?

(Ignore overhead for now. The cost of labor is where the opportunity for cost savings are significant, and this will the much larger cost bucket in terms of ongoing costs.)

Interviewee: Cost of labor is driven largely by compensation levels. We can get market research on comparative salaries in the U.S. and India or Malaysia for this job profile.

Firm: The per agent cost in North America is about $50,000 annually and about $5,000 in India or Malaysia.

Interviewee: That would imply that the cost of labor would go down by about 90 percent for this department, assuming it was all moved over. Still, the savings will not be quite that high, since the client will need some staff retained on site for quality monitoring, training, etc.—especially for the transition phase. And there will be other overhead costs per agent that we have not accounted for.

Firm: Yes, that's correct, but there is quite likely the potential for significant cost savings if we can make this work. Assume the client has decided there is enough financial incentive to try to go ahead. What are the next few steps the client needs to take?

Interviewee: The second area I wanted to explore was the operational aspect of offshore outsourcing. I want to understand what the high-level steps would

Visit the Vault Consulting Career Channel at www.vault.com/consulting — with insider firm profiles, message boards, the Vault Consulting Job Board and more.

VAULT CAREER LIBRARY   125

be that the client would have to execute to make this work and whether it has the expertise to do this or not. Has the client ever done any kind of outsourcing before?

Firm: No.

(You want to identify the different steps that the client would need to take, and you should do this in a systematic manner to make sure you don't miss important things. One way could be to think about the process chronologically— start from where the client is currently and moving toward the "to be" status, which is having the step outsourced. Think about the external changes [i.e. those dealing with the outsourcing partner] as well as the internal ones [e.g., handling possible staff layoffs].)

Interviewee: At this stage we have identified what the client could potentially outsource, but not the "how." The "how" would include steps such as selecting an appropriate outsourcing partner from a pool of candidates, developing an appropriate contract and other service level agreements, working with them to identify the best way to migrate the clients processes to the partner's systems, things such as databases procedures, etc. Then we would have to execute this, running a pilot phase to test everything, possibly running both our client and its outsourcing partner's systems in parallel during this phase. Finally, if all goes well, we would hand over the complete step to the outsourcing partner with appropriate quality checks in place. Internally, the client will need to develop policies and communication to deal with the changes—for example, around different HR requirements and possible layoffs, policies for having to work closely with a partner in a different time zone.

(A pilot phase will almost always take place before any major change to a business.)

Firm: So what is your final recommendation to the client?

Interviewee: I would recommend that it has the potential for reducing operating costs through outsourcing the debt collection agent's step. It needs to find an outsourcing partner to work with and should prefer one that has experience with this kind of outsourcing work, so the cost of training, systems migration, etc., are reduced and there is a higher probability of the change succeeding. It also needs to develop appropriate quality checking plans so it can monitor and control quality levels as it hands over part of its operations to its new partner. Simultaneously it needs to start planning for internal changes— for example, in its HR, which will take place if the outsourcing is executed.

Firm: Thank you.

© 2008 Vault.com Inc.

Case analysis

This case takes the concept of outsourcing, which is now commonplace in the IT industry, and pairs it with a financial service. The core question deals with assessing a particular business model to see if it can be made to work for the client, and what is required to do this. As mentioned previously, regardless of the industry, you need to understand the business model before being able to do any kind of analysis on it. Given how common outsourcing has become, it is quite reasonable for the interviewer to expect you to be familiar with it.

It is important not to think in buckets when making business decisions. In this kind of decision there are elements of finance, operations, change management and quality control that are key areas of the business you should be thinking of to evaluate the decision in a holistic manner. You may not hit all of the areas in your interview, nor would you go in depth in all (depending on the length of the interview), but only identifying one or two would not reflect favorably on your ability to think across functions. While it is important to look for different ways to make a positive business decision, do not hesitate to provide your interviewer with a negative conclusion to what the client is thinking about. In this case, it was unnecessary, given the obvious step that had potential to save on labor costs—but this will not always be the case.

PetCo Revenue Case

Your client, PetCo, is a pet food company in the United States. It has recently hired a new CEO to replace the retiring CEO with a mandate to drive revenue. Revenue has remained relatively flat for the past five years in the matured pet food industry. The CEO is under tremendous pressure from the board to grow its revenue by $600 million from the current revenue of $2 billion within the next year.

You have been hired to evaluate the feasibility of this goal. You have to assess whether the CEO can achieve the goal set by the board, and the options the CEO should consider.

Question: How can PetCo increase its revenue from $2 billion to $2.6 billion in the next year?

The following **background data** will be provided only if the interviewee asks for it:

• PetCo is one the largest players in the U.S. pet food industry, with 40 percent market share.

• Two other pet food companies have 8 percent market share each and the rest of the industry is highly fragmented, with all other companies having 1 to 2 percent of the market.

• One of the pet food companies with 8 percent market share is part of a larger food conglomerate, and it is looking to divest the pet food business. This particular pet food business focuses on birds and hamsters/gerbils.

• There will be minimal antitrust issues if a company in the pet food industry has less than 50 percent of the market share after acquisitions.

• The pet food industry in the U.S. is matured and will grow at 3 percent for the next year.

• PetCo, the company, is in a more favorable market position as the market leader and therefore, organic growth is projected to be higher at 5 percent for next year.

• PetCo products are mainly targeted at the two most common pets—cats and dogs—with very little presence in the pet food market for fish, birds and hamsters/gerbils. However, PetCo has always been interested in getting into the market for one of the less popular pets such as fish.

• The needs of less popular pets, especially fish, are not as well met as those of cats and dogs due to the poor offerings from the very small players.

• PetCo will be launching an innovative product this year by leveraging on its current R&D and distribution reach for fish. The market for fish food is currently dominated by the fragmented market players but the needs of pet fish are not well met. This PetCo product launch will result in an incremental revenue benefit of 5 percent of current revenue in the next year.

Suggested approach

The interviewee should attempt to determine the growth opportunities by establishing a clear framework using the four factors listed below. Looking to these four factors will help the interviewee to ask the right questions and form a big-picture perspective, while also providing opportunities to drill into details for other relevant information that will help answer the question.

The four factors are:

- Industry size and growth
- Company characteristics
- Customers' needs and profile
- Competitive dynamics

© 2008 Vault.com Inc.

- **Industry size and growth:** The interviewee must be able to determine the market size of the pet food industry by using the data of the PetCo market share (40 percent) and revenue ($2 billion). The market size of the pet food industry is therefore $5 billion (obtained by dividing $2 billion by 40 percent and multiplying by 100 percent). To evaluate the organic growth regardless of initiatives, the interviewee should know the growth rate of the pet food market in the U.S., which is 3 percent. By understanding that the market is growing at a rate slightly higher than inflation, the interviewee should be able to quickly assess that increased organic growth will definitely be inadequate in meeting the revenue target.

- **Company characteristics:** The interviewee should realize that PetCo, as such a large and significant market player, will have a wider distribution reach, better negotiation power with retailers and stronger marketing economies of scale, and is therefore more likely to exceed the overall market growth rate. The interviewee will likely be provided with the company organic growth rate of 5 percent once he is able to assess why the company organic growth rate for PetCo is higher than the market average. The interviewee will then calculate that the organic revenue growth of PetCo is $100 million, which is 5 percent multiplied by current revenue of $2 billion. The interviewee will continue to realize that organic growth will not help the CEO in achieving his mandate.

- **Customers' needs and profile:** The interviewee needs to quickly assess the most popular pets in the U.S., and ask whether their needs are already met. He will be informed that the needs of the most popular pets—cats and dogs—are already well satisfied by PetCo. However, the needs of fish are not as well met by the fragmented pet food companies in the market. This void provides an opportunity for PetCo to launch its innovative fish product, leveraging on its distribution reach, R&D and market research capabilities. The interviewee will be provided with the incremental revenue from the launch, which is 5 percent of the current revenue. A quick calculation will yield incremental revenue of $100 million. Ideally, the interviewee should conduct a quick sanity check to determine if a new production launch can capture $100 million in the first year.

- **Competitive dynamics:** The interviewee must seek to understand the competitive landscape of the pet food market, in particular that there are two smaller players with 8 percent share in the market. By expressing the desire to learn more about the two smaller players, the interviewee will be informed that one of the smaller players is owned by a large food conglomerate looking to divest its pet food business, and is currently focused on the bird and hamster/gerbil business. This smaller company's focus on birds and hamsters/gerbils is comple-

Visit the Vault Consulting Career Channel at **www.vault.com/consulting** — with insider firm profiles, message boards, the Vault Consulting Job Board and more.

VAULT CAREER LIBRARY   129

mentary to PetCo, whose current focus is cats, dogs and fish. An acquisition of the company will provide another incremental $400 million in revenue, because the acquired company has an 8 percent market share in a $5 billion market.

• This framework enables the interviewee to ask the right questions as additional new information is obtained from each of the factors in the framework. This information will help the interviewee drive towards developing the strategic initiatives of 30 percent revenue growth within an extremely short time frame of one year.

Basic recommendations

Given the industry evolution and PetCo market position, it is likely that the CEO will be able to achieve the goal of increasing incremental revenue by $600M within the next year through three strategic initiatives.

• First, organic growth due to PetCo's leading market position, wider distribution reach, better negotiation power with retailers and stronger marketing economies of scale will result in a 5 percent market-driven growth with net incremental revenue of $100 million (5 percent of $2 billion revenue = $100 million)

• Second, innovation-driven growth, spearheaded by PetCo's new product for the pet fish market will net a 5 percent incremental revenue benefit of $100 million (5 percent of $2 billion revenue = $100 million)

• Third, acquiring one of the smaller competitors with 8 percent of the market will immediately bring incremental revenue of $400 million (8 percent of $5 billion pet food market = $400 million)

Additional recommendations

The interviewee should also proactively address the following risks to provide a more comprehensive and well-thought-through recommendation.

• New product introduction—Reliable market research and pilot tests should be conducted to ensure successful pet fish product introduction with minimal cannibalization due to the current product focus of PetCo (cats and dogs) and the acquired firm (birds and hamsters/gerbils).

• For the innovation-driven growth, it is also necessary to do a sanity check to determine if the $100 million incremental revenue growth from launching a new product is feasible. Given that the entire pet food market is $5 billion, capturing 2 percent of the entire market from the rest of the competitors seems reasonable. Given that PetCo is going to acquire the smaller pet food company that focused on birds and gerbils/hamsters, there will be minimal cannibalization from launching a product for pet fish.

- Acquisition—Given that the new combined PetCo will have 48 percent of the pet food market, it is critical to address the concerns of the government regulator to ensure that it will not block the acquisition due to antitrust concerns.

Study notes

- A common mistake is to be too detail-oriented and not strategic in evaluating the options available to the CEO. It is easy to be overly focused on improving the capabilities of the company, for example, through increasing distribution and selling the same product at lower prices to generate increased volume. But this strategy will still not be sufficient to achieve the very aggressive growth target within the very short target time frame.

- The interviewee must quickly state that organic growth will not be able to satisfy the CEO's mandate. It is critical to take a step back and zero in on strategic sources of revenue growth, namely innovation-driven growth through new market penetration and acquisitions.

- All the revenue opportunities must add up to an incremental revenue growth of $600 million to answer the question. The interviewee might drive the case and get all the math correct, but still not ace it because of the failure to circle back to the question to answer the case.

Pro Bono Case

One of our pro bono engagements involves a nonprofit organization called Youth Inspiration (YI). YI's mission is the promotion of youth leadership, and its most popular program is its Leaders Day event, where speakers are invited to motivate and inspire young people. The event has been very well received, and is motivating students to take on leadership roles and responsibilities.

Youth Inspiration has held two LD events targeting middle school children in a midsized city, with around 4,000 students participating in each event for the past two years since its inception. YI uses volunteers to run the event, and no meals are provided for the students. Due to its limited fund-raising capability, the NPO projected that corporate sponsorship can cover 25 percent of the cost, while 75 percent must come from ticket sales. The speakers are not paid.

Visit the Vault Consulting Career Channel at www.vault.com/consulting — with insider firm profiles, message boards, the Vault Consulting Job Board and more.

VAULT CAREER LIBRARY   131

The executive director (ED) is looking to expand the Leaders Day event into the high school market, and has asked us whether its makes strategic and financial sense.

Firm: What do you think is the main cost structure of holding such an event? What must Youth Inspiration do to ensure profitability?

Interviewee: The main cost structure can be divided into fixed and variable costs. The fixed costs include rental of the venue and audiovisual equipment. The variable costs include transportation and food expense for the volunteers. Therefore, since the cost of the venue is fixed, it is critical for YI to fill it with as many students as it can.

Firm: Assume the rental cost of the venue and audiovisual equipment is $75,000, and the ratio of volunteers to students is 1:100, and the cost of providing meals and transportation to the volunteer is $25. Also, assume 80 percent of the seats will be sold. What is the break-even price given that there are 5,000 seats in the venue? Round up your final ticket price per student to the nearest dollar.

Interviewee: The number of seats to be sold to break even will be 4,000. The number of volunteers needed is 4,000/100 = 40. The volunteers will incur costs of $1,000. The total cost to be covered through ticket sales is ($75,000 + $1,000)*75 percent = $57,000 as 25 percent of the cost will be sponsored. The break-even price of each ticket should be at least $57,000/4,000 = $14.25 or $15.

Firm: Will you price the ticket at $15? Explain your rationale.

Interviewee: From the cost pricing perspective, this break-even price only reflects the cost of running the event with corporate sponsorship. This does not include the allocated salary cost of the ED and other full-time staff members' time in running Leaders Day, and also the time spent seeking corporate sponsorship. The "true" break-even ticket price should definitely be higher, which can be determined from a detailed cost accounting analysis.

From the market pricing perspective, it is important to determine the willingness of the student or school to pay for the event, which is significantly influenced by competitive or comparable offerings. If there are very similar events at a much higher or lower price, then YI can price according to the competition, but $15 is definitely the lower-end amount.

Firm: Tell me in more detail what you mean by competitive or comparable offerings.

Interviewee: Both the public and private sectors can offer comparable offerings. Within the public sector, education-related government agencies may organize interschool forums where motivational speakers give lectures. Within the private sector, for-profit companies can pay speakers to organize similar interschool forums. Straddling the private and public sector, other nonprofits can always organize similar events.

Firm: There is not much competition to YI's LD. Why do you think that is so?

Interviewee: In terms of the public sector, it may be hard to justify spending on the venue and speakers. Education-related government agencies may not see such a forum as a priority and, given limited resources, would rather focus their spending on more tangible items, such as improving infrastructure and teacher compensation.

Private companies may find it challenging to attract motivational speakers who do not want to be perceived as financially benefiting from speaking to young students. Speakers will usually be willing to speak to financially independent adults for a fee, but speaking to young students for a fee may have negative implications for their image.

The market for this type forum may already be saturated in terms of number of students, which explains why YI may not have strong competition from other nonprofits.

Firm: How do you determine if the market is already saturated? Assume that one million people live within the two-hour driving radius to the intended venue. It is almost impossible to convince schools to send students to an event more than two hours away. You should feel comfortable rounding your calculations to the nearest thousand.

Interviewee: The two previous Leaders Day events have already attracted 8,000 middle school students. We need to determine how many middle school students are in a typical population of one million people. Middle school consists of children in grades six, seven and eight, which covers ages from 12 to 15. We assume that everyone from age 12 to 15 is attending middle school. First, assume the typical life expectancy is 70 years old, so each age bucket is one million divided by 70. The total middle school population will be $(1,000,000/7)*3 = 43,000$.

Given that that there are a greater number of younger individuals than older in a typical population pyramid, 43,000 is a conservative estimate and the lower end. Therefore, having approximately 20 percent of the market means that YI has already penetrated the middle school market quite effectively.

Firm: If the current pricing for a middle school student is $15 for the event, does this translate into a financially sustainable situation? The ED is paid $60,000 and a full-time staff member is paid $40,000. The two Leaders Day

Visit the Vault Consulting Career Channel at **www.vault.com/consulting** — with insider firm profiles, message boards, the Vault Consulting Job Board and more.

VAULT CAREER LIBRARY 133

events contribute 80 percent of total revenue to YI. The other 20 percent of the revenue comes from 100 percent fee paying leadership workshops, where the only cost is from the ED and full-time staff salaries.

Interviewee: A $15 ticket price means that the revenue generated from sales is $15*8,000 = $120,000. Corporate sponsorship contributes 25 percent of the cost base for the two LD, which is $76,000*25 percent*2 = $38,000. The total revenue from the two LDs is $158,000. Given that the two LDs contribute 80 percent of total revenue, the total will be $158,000/80*100 = $198,000.

The total cost of one LD is $76,000. Therefore, the total cost to the nonprofit is $76,000*2+$60,000+$40,000 = $252,000.

YI is expected to lose $54,000 every year if the status quo prevails, and this situation is not financially viable.

Firm: What can YI do to overcome these financial challenges?

Interviewee: We can address the issue from both cost and revenue perspectives. From a cost perspective, the ED can reduce his or her salary, layoff the part-time staff, and look for a less expensive venue for the event. However, none of these options are helpful in ensuring YI's long-term success. Therefore, from a revenue perspective, the decision by the ED to enter the high school market is a strategic, financially sound decision.

Firm: Can you determine the break-even analysis for entering the high school market with one LD per year, and whether it is feasible? Assume that we can charge $30 a ticket for high school students, and that there is no corporate sponsorship. Assume the venue and volunteer costs are the same as the middle school LD.

Interviewee: YI is expected to lose $54,000 every year. Therefore, entering the high school market must ensure at least a $54,000 profit.

Let x be the number of students attending each event. The total cost will be $70,000+x/100. The total revenue will be (x*$30). The number of students is equal to $30x-$70,000-x/100 = $54,000. Therefore $30x-x/100 = $124,000 => $3,000x-x = $12,400,000 => x = 12,400,000/2,999 = 4,135, which is the break-even number.

The break-even number for attending high school students is 4,135 per LD.

Firm: What is your recommendation to the ED?

Interviewee: The ED should definitely look into entering the high school market. Currently, breaking even requires 4,135 high school students, each paying $30

 © 2008 Vault.com Inc.

for each LD. This break-even number is reasonable, given that the high school population is larger than the middle school population, due to the wider age ranges.

To ensure that the high school-focused LD can attract a reasonably large crowd, the ED can consider lowering the price by attaining some corporate sponsorship and leveraging its track record.

If Youth Inspiration is able to hold a second LD, then it will be able to generate at least $50,000 in profit and build financial reserves. The ED and full-time staff members must leverage the volunteer network to run an additional two events.

One key challenge may be YI's ability to attract high-quality speakers for all four events in a year, and therefore, there is a need to request referrals from current speakers or to cast the net wider to attract a greater number of speakers.

Publishing Company M&A Case

A large, global publishing company has hired us to help it with its M&A strategy. The company had a lot of M&A activity in the last 10 years, and a new CEO has come in to ask us to help him reevaluate that activity. How would you structure that?

Additional information provided during questioning

• The client is a large, global publishing company with holdings in a variety of markets internationally and with holdings in several industries. A full breakout of the company's holdings is included in Exhibit 1 (which should be given to the interviewee once he or she asks for more details on the client's holdings).

• The new CEO is a new client to the firm. The firm is hoping to establish a longer-term consulting relationship with the client. The new CEO is also the great-grandson of one of the founders of the company. When the company was originally founded, it was a railway industry reporting company; however, it made its name in the business news reporting industry. Given this information, the new CEO would likely be very reluctant to sell off his family's company's founding assets, like the professional publishing companies.

• The company is best known for its consumer and educational publishing assets in the U.S. and the U.K. Overseas, its brand is less category-specific, and its overseas businesses are growing faster than its U.S. businesses.

This is a three C's + market setting/dynamics case. A successful interviewee will find out/ask about the company's assets very early on in the case. The ex-

Visit the Vault Consulting Career Channel at **www.vault.com/consulting** — with insider firm profiles, message boards, the Vault Consulting Job Board and more.

VAULT CAREER LIBRARY

135

hibits are used both to give the interviewee information about the case and to test the interviewee's ability to sort and analyze qualitative and quantitative data, the crux of many strategy cases.

An advanced interviewee might bring up portfolio theory to evaluating the M&A strategy going forward, but that would only be expected of a business school graduate.

Breakdown of solution

Interviewee: So, it sounds like we've been brought in by a new CEO to re-evaluate this publishing company's holdings and recommend an M&A strategy going forward. Is that correct?

Firm: Yes, that's correct. How might you structure that kind of analysis?

Interviewee: Can I have a few minutes to collect my thoughts?

Firm: Of course. Just let me know when you're ready to begin.

(Few minutes go by ...)

Interviewee: Well, I would want to divide my analysis into four major buckets: 1) What are the company's core capabilities and interests?; 2) What are the market dynamics like in the markets that the client currently has business in—are they attractive, or unattractive markets?; 3) Who are the client's customers in each line of business and are there revenue synergies and cross-selling opportunities for those customers between businesses?; 4) What's the competition like for each of the businesses that we're in? Where is the competition beating us, and where are we likely to beat the competition?

(A high-level summary of how to approach the case in this way is on page 137.)

© 2008 Vault.com Inc.

COMPANY

What's in our portfolio?
- What lines of business? What industries do we play in? What customer groups do we serve?
- What geographic markets are we located in?
  Where are there cost synergies to be had within the portfolio?
    What are our core capabilities?
    What are we best known for?

CUSTOMERS

Who are the customers for each of the businesses?
Are there any revenue synergies to be had between businesses?
- What are those revenue synergies and how much are they worth?

COMPETITORS

- Who are our competitors?
- What do we have that differentiates us from our competition?
- Where are our competitors strong? Where are we stronger than them? (Market shares?) What markets/industries are we losing to the competition in?

MARKET SETTING/ DYNAMICS

- What markets are growing? What markets are shrinking?
- What markets that we are in have good barriers to entry?
- Are there attractive markets adjacent to the markets that we're currently in that we might like to enter?
- What markets carry the most risk for our businesses?

Firm: Let's begin with your questions about the company. What would you like to know most?

Interviewee: Sure. I'd actually like to know a little more about both this new CEO and the company's holdings. If the client has been doing a lot of M&A activity in the last 10 years, I imagine that it has a lot of different lines of business—can I get a better sense of that?

Firm: Sure. Both are good topics to have a good understanding of. The client is a large, global publishing company with holdings in a variety of markets internationally and with holdings in several industries. A full breakout of the company's holdings is included in Exhibit 1.

Visit the Vault Consulting Career Channel at **www.vault.com/consulting** — with insider firm profiles, message boards, the Vault Consulting Job Board and more.

V/\ULT CAREER LIBRARY **137**

Exhibit 1: Client's Businesses

B2B Magazines and Newspapers	Web sites	Consumer Magazines
Shipping Monthly Magazine	Shipping.Com	This Month in Business
Chicken Farmer's Weekly Report	GlobalLawyer.Com	Your Health
Global Lawyer Magazine	Rail.Com	Women's Health
Corn Harvest Daily Report	HighSeas.com	Family Health
Gulf Stream Monthly	HealthCare Information.Com	
Gulf Coast Report	NewMedicalScience .Com	**B2B Rating Services**
Gulf Gazette	Science.Com	Small Business Ratings-U.S.
Railway Monthly	Hospital.Com	Small Business Ratings-Asia
Rail and Transport Report	AsiaLaw.Com	Snoody's Ratings
Railway News Daily	AfricaLaw.Com	
HealthGroup Quarterly	MiddleEastLaw.Com	**Consumer Publishing**
New MedicalScience Monthly	EuropeLaw.Com	Learning Tree Workbooks
Hospital Administrator News	AustraliaLaw.Com	Timeless Paperbacks
Crop & Grain Quarterly Report	TravelGroup.Com	Asia Paperbacks
Asia Law Review	Airway.Com	PanEuropa Paperbacks
New England Law Journal	AirTravel.Com	
Southwest Law Monthly	NationalLawyer.Com	**Educational Publishing**
Atlanta Lawyer	TravelAgent.Com	Watson Education
Cleveland Lawyer	GlobalShipper.Com	Watson Testing
National Hospital Administrator Report	NurseNews.Com	Watson Textbooks
	Doctor.Com	
	PhysicianAssistant. Com	
	ClevelandLawyer.Com	

© 2008 Vault.com Inc.

The company is best known for its consumer and educational publishing assets in the U.S. and the U.K. Overseas, its brand is less category-specific, and its overseas businesses are growing faster than its U.S. businesses.

In terms of the new CEO, there's a lot to know there, too. The CEO is a new client to the firm and is also the great-grandson of one of the founders of the company. When the company was originally founded, it was a railway industry reporting company; however, it made its name in the B2B news reporting industry. Given this, the new CEO would likely be very reluctant to sell off his family's company's founding assets, like the professional publishing companies.

Interviewee: That's good client background to have. I imagine that we're trying to impress this new CEO so that, if we do a good job with this project, we'll get more work.

Firm: We definitely are. The firm is hoping to establish a longer-term consulting relationship with the client. But that doesn't mean that we are just going to tell him what he wants to hear—we need to impress him with sharp, data-driven analysis. What are you most interested in looking at in your analysis given what you know now?

Interviewee: Right. Well, in looking at Exhibit 1, it looks like this is more than just a publishing company, even if that's what the company is best known for. It looks like it has a lot of web sites, and some other businesses, like ratings agencies.

Firm: That's right. It's gotten pretty diversified. Most of the web sites were purchased in the last five years of M&A activity. Let me give you some more data on the company's holdings:

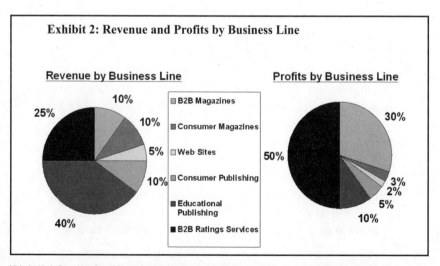

Exhibit 2: Revenue and Profits by Business Line

Revenue by Business Line

- 10% — B2B Magazines
- 25%
- 10% — Consumer Magazines
- 5% — Web Sites
- 10% — Consumer Publishing
- 40%
- Educational Publishing
- B2B Ratings Services

Profits by Business Line

- 30%
- 50%
- 3%
- 2%
- 5%
- 10%

Firm: What does this exhibit tell you?

Interviewee: It tells me a few things. First, it looks like the educational publishing business brings in a significant amount of the revenue, but only 10 percent of the profits. Second, it seems like the B2B ratings services, while small, bring in almost half of the profits. The story is very similar with the B2B magazines business. Third, it seems like the consumer magazines and publishing businesses are not the real drivers of profits for the company.

(Here, interviewees should make at least two observations from the data in Exhibit 2. If they do not get all of the observations listed above, that's fine, but the interviewer is entitled to push them to observe as many things as possible from the data before moving on.)

Firm: That's great. Now let me show you some more data that we put together for the case:

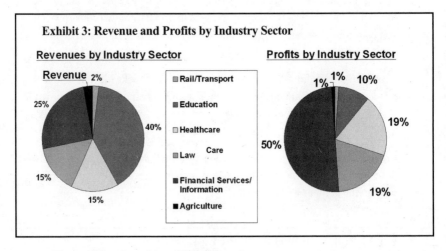

Exhibit 3: Revenue and Profits by Industry Sector

Firm: What does this exhibit tell you?

Interviewee: Let me make sure that I understand the difference between the two exhibits first. Exhibit 1 showed the company's revenue and profits by its lines of business, and Exhibit 2 shows the company's revenue and profits by the industry sectors that it's in. So, the web sites in the legal sector are in "Law" instead of in "Web Sites."

Firm: That's exactly right.

(The interviewer will likely make sure that the interviewee understands the difference between the two exhibits before analyzing the data—it's the same revenue and profits, just divided up and looked at in two difference ways.)

© 2008 Vault.com Inc.

Interviewee: Well, it tells me a couple of things. First, again, the education sector seems to make up a large portion of the revenue for the company—but not the profits. Second, it looks like the rail/transport sector doesn't make up a large portion of the revenue or the profits of the company. Agriculture doesn't look that necessary, or attractive either. Fourth, it looks like both the legal sector and the health care sector contribute significantly to both revenue and profits.

(Again, the interviewee should make at least two observations at this point— but should be pushed to come up with more, as this data will likely drive the case.)

Firm: That's right. So, I just have one more piece of data on the company that I'd like to know your thoughts on.

What does the exhibit below tell you?

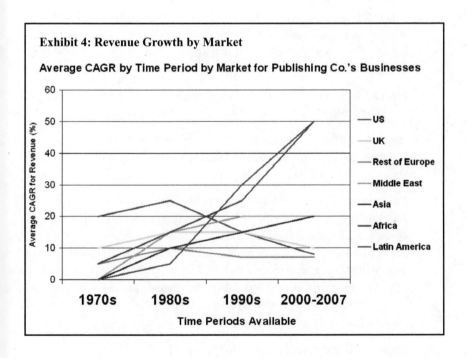

Exhibit 4: Revenue Growth by Market

Average CAGR by Time Period by Market for Publishing Co.'s Businesses

Interviewee: Well, I have to say that I'm not surprised. If I'm reading this correctly, this illustrates the growth rates for the company's businesses in different geographic markets for the last few decades.

Firm: Yes, that's correct.

Interviewee: Well, they also look similar to the relative growth rates for the GDPs of the countries in these regions for the last few decades. What I take from this in a nutshell is that the U.S., U.K. and European businesses are no longer growing nearly as fast as the businesses in developing parts of the world, like Latin America, Asia, Africa and the Middle East.

Firm: That's right. And you're right about it tying to GDP growth—why might that be?

(Answering this question will give an interviewee bonus points, but is not necessary for a successful case interview.)

Interviewee: Well, from the looks of these businesses, it seems like the client mainly serves B2B customers—and education customers. So, as long as there's healthy economic growth and development in a market, I imagine the businesses will do well, especially that ratings agency business, which probably really takes off when economies and capital markets start to develop.

Firm: That's right. We found that revenue growth for these businesses had a strong correlation with capital market development in a country.

Anyhow, let's say that you run into the CEO in the hallway at the client site, and he's eager to know how the case is going and what we're likely to recommend. How would you summarize this case?

Interviewee: Well, I would say that we've done a lot of analysis on the key revenue and profit drivers for his company, and that it looks like the company's business lines in B2B publishing and ratings services, particularly in the legal, health care and financial services sectors, drive a lot of the company's current profitability. Those businesses should definitely not be sold. Furthermore, if he's concerned with where he should make strategic acquisitions going forward, he should look to developing countries and markets, where his businesses are growing faster, as their economies are growing faster.

Firm: And what about the businesses he should sell?

Interviewee: Well, that's a tricky one. I mean, the rail/transport sector does not look that significant in terms of revenue or profits; so, it could easily be sold. But I know that this was this CEO's great-grandfather's business; so, if we're going to recommend that he sell it, I imagine that will be a hard sell, and

© 2008 Vault.com Inc.

one that I wouldn't necessarily try to make when I ran into the CEO in the hall-way.

Firm: That makes sense—and you're probably right. Good job!

(An advanced interviewee might bring up portfolio theory in the summary of which businesses to sell and which to keep, but that would only be expected of a business school graduate—and even then, probably only in a case interview for a corporate finance consulting practice.)

Regional Bank Commercial Case

Some case facts initially offered by the interviewer

• Super Bank is a regional bank in the Southeast with corporate/commercial operations in eight states.

• It has a separate charter in each state and banks in each state operate autonomously.

• Its rapid growth, lack of business focus and segmentation in commercial banking have contributed to commercial banking problems.

• It is unable to determine profitability, which is especially important to the bank's management.

• The objective is to make the corporate bank sought by customers, feared by competitors and a source of pride for employees.

Questions to be answered by candidate

If you were the engagement manager on this job, what would be your approach and potential solution?

Candidate evaluation

It is important the candidate understands and probes why the bank is in this position. Both quantitative and qualitative sides of the case need to be analyzed. There are multiple angles for this case. Some of the issues the candidate needs to address/assess are:

• The profitability question.

Visit the Vault Consulting Career Channel at **www.vault.com/consulting** — with in-sider firm profiles, message boards, the Vault Consulting Job Board and more.

V/\ULT CAREER LIBRARY   **143**

• The current image of the bank within its external and internal customers.
• Identify potential reasons for lack of high brand image, if any.
• Key question to answer in this case: issues of focus and whether the "Is bigger better?" philosophy works for Super Bank.

Suggested solutions

For answering the profitability question, one has to analyze the cost side and revenue sides of the client's banking operation.

Interviewee: What is the customer base of the bank across regions?

Firm: One million commercial customers.

Interviewee: What is the average size of a customer?

Firm: It has customers of all sizes.

Interviewee: Do we have any information about the spread?

Firm: Bank borrows from the Fed at a rate of 6 percent and lends money at 9 percent.

Interviewee: If we look at the cost side, what information is available?

Firm: Major cost comes from the credit officers, which totals $75,000,000 per year.

Interviewee: That's a huge cost. Does this vary according to the credit amount?

Firm: Each officer spends the same amount of time on each credit proposal, no matter what the size.

Interviewee: And how many are there at present?

Firm: Seven hundred and fifty credit officers.

Interviewee: If we look at the cost side again, what information is available on variable costs?

Firm: There's no exact figure for the entire bank at this point, but the industry average for similar operations is between 2 to 2.5 percent of the operational size.

Interviewee: That's interesting! Is there any information about the average balance per customer for the bank?

Firm: $50,000.

Possible analysis regarding profitability

© 2008 Vault.com Inc.

With the available information and some assumptions, the candidate can calculate the following:

Revenue = 3 percent (the spread - 9 percent to 6 percent) * 1,000,0000 (customer size) * $50,000 (average balance) = $1.5 billion

Costs are divided into variable costs (charge offs) and fixed costs (salary, rent etc.). Assuming the industry range, the variable costs can be charged at 2.5 percent of total deposits. Hence, variable costs are $50 billion (number of customers * average balance) * 2.5% = $1.25 million.

Therefore, the Contribution Margin is 20 percent. (Revenue - Variable Cost)/Revenue).

The candidate can further try to calculate the break-even volume of loans each officer must process in a year to justify the cost incurred:

Given that the spread is 9 percent - 6 percent = 3 percent, assume charge off is 2.5 percent

Therefore at break-even:

3 percent (X) = 2.5 percent (X) + $100,000 (cost spent on each credit officer).

X = $20 million = volume of business each person should handle each year.

Possible recommendation for profitability

This gives the interviewee a decent peek at the bank's profitability. A thorough study of its variable costs and fixed costs can be undertaken to come across a more accurate figure. The bank's management should also make a decision on whether the credit officers' costs are justifiable and whether they will be able to generate the required volume of business.

From the given information, one can also come to the conclusion that the bank is taking too many small loan applications. It should reduce the amount of time on small loans, increase the rate for small loans or exit the small loan business entirely.

Possible solutions for image-building among both external and internal customers

For analyzing the image question, the candidate can adopt the three Cs (company, customer and competition) analysis. Then he or she can probe to identify potential reasons for the bank's decline in customer service, if any.

Interviewee: The first issue I would like to address is why customers would want to come to this bank over others. Does it offer better rates or lower processing fees?

Visit the Vault Consulting Career Channel at **www.vault.com/consulting** — with insider firm profiles, message boards, the Vault Consulting Job Board and more.

VAULT CAREER LIBRARY   **145**

Firm: The bank's rates are very competitive and some of the lowest in the industry.

Interviewee: Do the customers face any other problems in terms of customer service?

Firm: Service time is a problem. Customers have to call a different phone number for each type of question or problem. Call wait times are often long.

Interviewee: Is there any reason why customers avoid this bank or the area where the bank wants to improve?

Firm: The bank has inconsistent credit underwriting skills, though it maintains good credit quality.

Interviewee: Is the inconsistency due to its many branches in different states adopting various processes for underwriting?

Firm: Yes, your guess is right. Also, cost and credit controls have tightened while the bank has actively acquired new banks, thereby complicating the commercial banking process.

Interviewee: Has there been any research on why the underwriting skills are inconsistent?

Firm: The bank is not providing a high quality of service to customers due to growing friction between the account officers, product units and credit administration.

Interviewee: Has there been a problem of workforce turnover within the bank?

Firm: Yes, the bank has not been able to attract and retain the best account officers.

Interviewee: Are these problems in one particular state or across locations?

Firm: In most of the states.

Interviewee: How competitive is the environment? Is there any bank operating in the same landscape in all locations?

Firm: There's no single bank within all states but there are a number of smaller local banks in every state that are highly competitive.

(From the above information the candidate can identify that due to expansion through acquisitions, the focus on commercial banking has been shaken and customers of the acquired banks in different states are suffering.)

Possible recommendation for customer service issue

© 2008 Vault.com Inc.

The following are some possibilities:

- To maintain uniformity and to improve quality of customer service, the bank needs to consolidate the commercial operations across all of the states in which it operates.

- Institute relationship managers and service managers to improve the quality of customer service. The company can consider a workforce restructure (e.g., adding more repair personnel or more technically knowledgeable staff to the help desk), as well as a job tracking system, which would allow the staffer to send a repair person familiar with that customer or type of system.

- Focus on the HR policy and make an effort to retain the best talent. Introduce performance-based incentive systems.

- Harmonize relationships and make sure there are formal communication channels between the account officers and credit administration.

One should question the implications of "market leader" status and recognize that customer service is often best conducted by smaller, more customer-focused organizations. One can also try to pinpoint what has recently changed in the industry (recent bankruptcies or acquisitions, etc.) and adopt policies accordingly.

The final part of analysis involves whether the bank needs to expand through acquisitions or consolidate its current operations. This is a demand-oriented question, and one can perform a SWOT analysis (strength, weakness, opportunities and threats) to formulate an answer.

Possible analysis

The candidate already has information from the above discussions. The situation can be quickly summarized as follows:

Strengths

- The bank has grown through multiple acquisitions.

- It has good credit writing skills and a good customer base.

- It has already established commercial banking skills.

Weakness

- There is a lack of established processes at this point, especially in determining profitability for the bank as a whole. Growing bigger without consoli-

Visit the Vault Consulting Career Channel at **www.vault.com/consulting** — with insider firm profiles, message boards, the Vault Consulting Job Board and more.

VAULT CAREER LIBRARY   147

dating existing operations will only make the banking operation more complicated.

• Quality of customer service and falling brand equity are issues.

Opportunities

• The absence of a single banking giant in the Southeast area.

• Once the bank's operations are consolidated and formalized, it will definitely have a competitive advantage and can expand its business.

Threats

More than threats, the bank must research the following before making any future acquisitions.

• The client must examine if any new acquisition would complement its existing competence and strategy (i.e., commercial banking, high growth or high profitability, etc.) and what purpose it would serve.

• The demographics of the area surrounding the prospective acquisition should be examined. Population, business concentration, income levels, etc., should be compared with those of historically successful banks. Location of competitors should also be considered.

Possible recommendation

• The bank should now concentrate on focus and aim to fulfill the objective of making the corporate bank sought by customers, feared by competitors and a source of pride for employees.

• At this point, "bigger is better" is not a viable solution, given that the profitability of the bank is not exceptionally good.

Key takeaways

This case can prove to be lengthy and very involved, given the three components that the candidate is expected to consider. It is not expected that an interviewee would cover all of the above topics, but rather work through selected topics in a logical fashion. It is important that the candidate pursues a solution that is holistic and understands the complete nature of the banking issues involved. The recommendations for improving customer service and for the issue of focus are a few possible solutions among many. The candidate may come up with his or her own ideas.

© 2008 Vault.com Inc.

Satellite Communications Systems Case

Your client is a high-tech engineering firm that provides engineering services in the satellite communications industry. The client's business has grown over the past decade through work subcontracted to it by global engineering firms that establish satellite communications systems in various countries. The client has developed a lot of cutting-edge technology as part of its work with these large multinationals and generally has a very good reputation in the industry. However, new contracts have dried up over the last 12 months, as the industry as a whole is going through a lean phase.

The client has decided to examine the satellite communications technologies it has developed to see if any of them can be put to further commercial benefit independent of specific contracts. If so, the client would need further advice on how to extract this commercial value. How would you advise your client?

(This case has several components to it. You need to assess if the client has anything that might have commercial value, what the market for it might be and whether the client has the resources to make the two meet. You will need some understanding of the industry and also the current lean phase it is going through.)

Interviewee: Could you begin by giving me some background on the satellite communications industry? I'd like to better understand where our client fits into it.

(The interviewer will not be expecting you to have any specific knowledge of an industry and so with several different areas to examine, it is usually a good idea to start investigating at a high level.)

Firm: Satellite communications networks have three to four major components ranging from ground services, uplinking, downlinking, integration software and so on. Each is highly specialized and a mini industry of its own, comprised of different companies providing engineering services with usually very little overlap. The large global engineering firms are the ones that win contracts from states, countries, national telecom firms, etc., and then subcontract out different parts to these specialized firms. Our client is one such firm. It provides customized software for different parts of the network that is used to interconnect the different hardware components that other engineering firms provide so that the communications data can flow through them.

Interviewee: So would it be correct to say that all the technologies that the client is currently reviewing for commercial potential are software-based?

Visit the Vault Consulting Career Channel at **www.vault.com/consulting** — with insider firm profiles, message boards, the Vault Consulting Job Board and more.

VAULT CAREER LIBRARY **149**

Firm: Yes, that's correct. The client writes the software that makes different pieces of hardware work together to transmit communication data around the whole system.

(You now know a little about the industry and where the client fits in. You should try to structure your work to move forward. Take a few minutes to think about the best way to do this.)

Interviewee: I would like to use the following structure going forward. I need to understand what the client's product might be and who the potential customers are. I'd like to understand if these customers are all going to be from the satellite communications industry and, if this is the case, how they are affected by the current lean phase. After understanding the product and its potential customers, I'd like to know what is involved in bringing this product to them, or, in other words, what would be required to bring the product to market. I would need to understand the market itself—aspects of it like sales channels, marketing, pricing, competitor offerings and so on. All of this will help develop an assessment of whether the client has a competitive product offering it can bring to the market in a profitable way.

Firm: That sounds reasonable. Where would you like to begin?

Interviewee: I'd like to start with the product itself. To reiterate, the client's product consists of pieces of software that it has developed over the last several years. So far, has it been providing this software to its customers when it receives a contract?

Firm: No. The software has almost always been developed as part of the contract and for the specific client. Do you think this will affect the company in any way going forward?

(Anything developed specifically as part of a contract for a customer may have issues surrounding who owns the work. In other words, the intellectual property rights for such technology will depend on what has been agreed to and stated in the contract. This is not specific to technology industries and applies elsewhere as well. The client will only be able to commercialize technologies it owns the rights to or that it can gain the rights to from whomever it was developed for. It's definitely worth exploring to understand what the status is with respect to this.)

Interviewee: If the technologies were developed as part of contracts, we need to first assess who owns the rights to them. The client will only be able to use those technologies it owns or can get the rights to. Do we know the status of the rights to the technologies it has developed in this respect?

   © 2008 Vault.com Inc.

Firm: That's a good point you raise and it will be something that will have to be examined. How would you propose doing this?

Interviewee: For each piece of software that the client is examining, we would need to review the contract under which it was developed to see what it states about the intellectual property rights, and decide on a case-by-case basis. We may need formal legal advice to do this.

Firm: That's correct. Assume for now that the client has rights to some of the technologies and can essentially bundle them into a software package similar to, for example, a Windows CD in a computer store. How would you next proceed?

Interviewee: The next step is to understand who the customers might be. At this point my assumption is that given this is very specialized work, the customer base is largely from the satellite communications industry, or the same companies with whom the client generally contracts. Is this a correct assumption?

(You will need to make assumptions as you move through the case to push forward. It is important, however, to state when you are making an assumption and ask the interviewer if he or she agrees with it. If not, he or she may point you in a different direction.)

Firm: Yes, that's correct.

(If all potential customers belong to this industry, it is likely most are affected by its current lean phase. You need to be creative here to see if there is a way for the client to repackage its offering in a manner that is different from current conditions. There can be different ways of approaching this. You should try to describe your approach in more than just one line so that the interviewer fully understands what you are suggesting.)

Interviewee: The issue that I am seeing as a potential roadblock is that the industry slowdown that is forcing our client to re-examine its product affects the same customers it would approach under any new business model. However, I am wondering if the client's product can be offered in a different format at a lower cost to its customers. For example, perhaps the software can be broken into different components that can be sold to different hardware companies at a lower price compared to a package for entire systems. This would also refocus the client's customer base from consisting of only the major engineering firms to any hardware vendor wanting its equipment to be able to communicate with other vendors' hardware, thereby increasing the potential number of customers.

(A positive response from the interviewer will tell you that you are following a path that could potentially work or is at least worth exploring. Unless you are ex-

Visit the Vault Consulting Career Channel at **www.vault.com/consulting** — with insider firm profiles, message boards, the Vault Consulting Job Board and more.

V/\ULT CAREER LIBRARY **151**

ceptionally sure of the idea you have brought up, a neutral to negative response should suggest the interviewer wants you to consider a different approach.)

Firm: That's an interesting suggestion. It is quite possible that the market is still receptive to lower cost pieces of a system rather than a full-blown network and you are correct, it would potentially broaden your customer base as well. How would you explore this further?

(Any business decision hinges in large part on quantifying the costs and benefits involved and it is important to investigate them as part of any recommendation. Your interviewer may or may not require it, but you need to show that you can handle the numbers involved if required.)

Interviewee: It would be important to quantify this as a potential opportunity so that any decisions made are not just based on gut feeling. My next step in exploring this would be to match pieces of software that can be sold independently to companies that are potential customers. This will help develop some sort of market sizing estimate. Do we have any information relevant to this?

Firm: The client has not worked through any numbers as yet, since it does not know whether any such breakdown of its software is even possible. At this early stage it is just trying to get a high-level understanding of what the end-to-end process might look like. Assuming there is a big enough market to make this worthwhile, what would you advise them to do next?

(Do a mental recap of the analysis structure you proposed to see where you are. The interviewer has more than likely kept the structure you proposed in the back of his or her mind and will want to see that you are using it—if you need to drastically deviate from it, that's OK, but let the interviewer know you are doing this and why.)

Interviewee: So far we have determined there is a product the company can put together and despite the overall industry going through a lean phase there is a market for this product due to its lower cost. I would next like to understand details of the market to assess what the client needs to do to bring such an offering to the market, and if the client has the necessary resources to do so. I would like to initially look at competitor offerings, pricing strategies and channels to place the product, but may need to look at other things as well as we move ahead.

(It's good to leave the door open for anything that you may think of later.)

Firm: Let's ignore pricing and competitors for now and focus on channels for introducing the product to market. What channels would you suggest the client explore for launching such a product?

© 2008 Vault.com Inc.

(Here is another opportunity to show some creativity. Remember though that the client will be launching to a narrow range of customers. One way to think about it in a structured manner is to keep different kinds of media types (print, audio-visual, electronic, etc.) in mind. Think about which ones might be appropriate and have suitable examples for each of them.)

Interviewee: Given that the client is targeting a very specific customer base, I would hypothesize they do not need a mass campaign. Rather they should focus on channels that are narrow but relevant for companies in this specific industry. Such channels could include trade magazines and journals in the print media; industry trade fairs where the client's representatives can speak to several companies as well as direct mailers and a road show to the major firms for more one-on-one interaction and sales pitches.

Firm: I think that's reasonable. Thank you.

Case analysis

This case requires you to go through the steps of thinking about the possibility of repackaging an existing product and launching it afresh in the market. You develop the case by moving through decisions on several smaller components. For example you have to decide if there is any product to support the new business model under consideration, if there is a reasonable market for it, what channels could be used to bring the product to market and so on. The analysis would be incomplete if you did not consider these components individually and use decisions about each of them as building blocks for the overall issue. This highlights the need for a good initial structure to be sure you cover most if not all the important areas that could influence such a decision.

The case could have become far more quantitative at several points. For example, when proposing to break up the product offering into smaller pieces and offer it to the market at lower cost, the interviewer could have chosen to make this into a market sizing-related case, where you might need to calculate such things as revenue potential. Do not become nervous or concerned about your unfamiliarity with the industry, as interviewers will not expect you to have specific knowledge about it. What they will expect is for you to be able to abstract out of the situation the business decisions and structured thinking that need to be applied, and then hone in to use case and industry specific facts (which are uncovered during the course of the interview) to refine your analysis and recommendations.

Specialty Kitchenware Brand Case

A private equity firm client is considering buying the U.S. distribution rights to a brand of European specialty kitchenware. The asking price for the distribution rights is $10 million. The kitchenware brand up for sale is not currently sold in the U.S. The client has hired our firm to advise on whether or not this is a good idea. How would you structure our response?

Additional information provided during questioning

• The client is a typical private equity (PE) firm. It usually makes investments for no more than five years. It is a N.Y.-based firm. The client typically makes investments of no more than $10 million dollars. The client does not have any other holdings in the kitchenware mark—this is a new market for it, and that's one of the reasons why it has hired us.

• In order for the PE client to purchase the rights, it needs to be able to grow revenue for the brand to $50 million in five years.

• Not much is known about the specialty kitchenware market in the U.S. There are no analyst reports on the market, its trends or growth rates. The brand up for sale consists of cookware, ceramics, pots, pans and specialty utensils priced at $40 to $500 apiece.

Suggested high-level overview of solution

This is a three Cs case—with the "company" and "customer" Cs tailored to this specific case—which is easily analyzed with a quick market-sizing exercise. Numbers really drive the answer, and the interviewee needs to remember that this is a PE firm—if the numbers are not achievable quickly, it's not a good buy for the firm.

There is one "brainstorming" exercise, in which an interviewee can demonstrate his or her creativity in finding data, which is always a helpful skill for a consultant.

Breakdown of solution (including quantitative analyses and qualitative evaluations)

Interviewee: So, let me just make sure that I understand the case: The client is a private equity firm, and it has hired us to help it decide whether to buy the

U.S. distribution rights to a specialty kitchenware line. The asking price is $10 million. Is that correct?

Firm: Yes. That's right.

Interviewee: Before I collect my thoughts, does the PE firm specialize in bringing European brands to the U.S., or in kitchenware?

Firm: Those are good questions. The answer is that it does not. The client is a typical private equity firm. It usually makes investments for no more than five years. It is a N.Y.-based firm. The client typically makes investments of no more than $10 million dollars. The client firm does not have any other holdings in the kitchenware market—this is a new market for it, and that's one of the reasons why it hired us.

Interviewee: Great. Do you mind if I take a few minutes to collect my thoughts?

Firm: Not at all. Take your time.

(Few minutes go by ...)

Interviewee: I have three main topics that I'd like to analyze to make a decision on buying these rights: 1) the product line/brand, 2) consumers/retailers in the specialty kitchenware, and overall kitchenware market in the U.S., and 3) the competition in the kitchenware market. I divided the key questions for my analysis in those as follows:

BRAND/PRODUCT LINE	• What is the product offering that we're buying? What's its price range? How differentiated would it be in the market? • What's the brand awareness in the U.S. right now?
CONSUMERS/ RETAILERS	• How many consumers are there for this sort of product? Is the consumer base growing in the U.S.? • How much are consumers willing to pay for this product? • How many retailers are there for this product line? How much do they need it?
COMPETITION	• How much competition is there in the market? • Is the competition likely to increase or decrease in the near future?

Visit the Vault Consulting Career Channel at **www.vault.com/consulting** — with in-sider firm profiles, message boards, the Vault Consulting Job Board and more.

VAULT CAREER LIBRARY   **155**

Firm: That's a great way to start. In terms of your questions about the market, I have some not-so-great news: Not much is known about the specialty kitchenware market in the U.S. There are no analyst reports on the market, its trends or growth rates. The brand up for sale consists of cookware, ceramics, pots, pans and specialty utensils priced at $40 to $500 apiece—quite expensive. But the margins are great on the product; so, that's why the client is interested in it.

Interviewee: That answers a lot of my questions about the brand/product line. Do we know much about consumers or the competition in the market?

Firm: Not really—that's a big part of why the client hired us. And that brings me to my next question: What kind of research would you do to find out about the market and to answer some of the key questions that you've defined?

(This is the brainstorming exercise. An interviewee should come up with three to four ways/data sources that they might look to find out about the market. A more exhaustive list, included below, is divided up by the key buckets of information that the interviewee already outlined.)

Interviewee: I can think of several data sources that might answer some of my questions. Other than analyst reports, which you've already said don't really exist for this market, I can think of using lit searches on the specialty kitchenware market in the U.S., trade journals on kitchenware, consumer and market data on the brand and product line in Europe from the company that the client is considering buying the rights from, primary research on shelf space devoted to high-end kitchenware in key retailers (like Bed, Bath and Beyond, Williams-Sonoma, Crate & Barrel, etc.), analyst and annual reports on cookware retailers in the U.S., analyst and annual reports on cookware manufacturers in the U.S., and interviews or surveys with cookware consumers in the U.S.

© 2008 Vault.com Inc.

(The following is a more detailed and compartmentalized list of the above, but really, a brainstormed list like the one above is fine for an exercise like this in a case interview.)

COMPETITION

- Lit search on brand/product line in Europe
- Lit search on cookware brands/products in the U.S.
- Trade journals on cooking, cookware, kitchenware
- Product line/brand info from company in Europe

CONSUMERS/ RETAILERS

- Primary research in/visits to cookware retailers (C&B, Williams-Sonoma, BB&B) to measure shelf space allocations
- Consumer data on brand consumers in Europe
- Interviews/surveys with consumers in the U.S.
- Annual reports/analyst reports on cookware retailers in the U.S.

BRAND/PRODUCT LINE

- Lit searches on cookware manufacturers in the U.S.
- Analyst and annual reports on cookware manufacturers in the U.S.
- Trade journals on cookware/kitchenware
- Shelf-space analysis in cookware retailers

Firm: That's great, and a really good list of potential data sources. Now, in order for the PE client to purchase the rights, it needs to be able to grow revenue for the brand to $50 million in five years. Knowing that, how would you decide if it's a good idea to buy the rights?

Interviewee: Well, I would need to know the size of the current specialty kitchenware market and estimate how much of that market I think this new brand could get in five years.

Firm: That's right. What would you size the market at?

(The following market sizing is illustrative but is not the only market sizing that would be reasonable. An interviewee should definitely know the assumptions that the U.S. has a population of 275 to 300 million and that there are approximately 100 million households in the U.S.—those are considered common knowledge for case interviews. Other than that, an interviewee should feel free to make assumptions that are reasonable in order to get to a "back of the envelope" market size. The main piece of advice is that the interviewee should make assumptions, but check in with the interviewer on whether those assumptions are reasonable.)

Visit the Vault Consulting Career Channel at **www.vault.com/consulting** — with insider firm profiles, message boards, the Vault Consulting Job Board and more.

VAULT CAREER LIBRARY   **157**

Interviewee: Because kitchenware is purchased on a household basis, I'd like to size the market in terms of households, instead of in terms of individual consumers.

Firm: That seems like a good idea.

Interviewee: I know that the U.S. has approximately 100 million households. Let's assume that while most all of those households are consumers of the cookware market, most are not consumers of the specialty or high-end kitchenware market. Let's assume that only about 10 percent of households would be the consumers that we should be interested in. Is that fair?

Firm: Yeah, that's about right—it's a little bigger than that, and I think that we're hoping to grow the market, why don't we use 20 percent?

Interviewee: Great—20 percent then; so, there are about 20 million households that we're concerned with. Now, I'm going to assume that since specialty kitchenware is probably a fairly durable good …

Firm: Yes, it is—for the prices that these spatulas sell for!

Interviewee: Yes, so, I'm going to assume that those 20 million households probably only make a specialty cookware purchase once every five years. So, in any given year, only about four million households are purchasing.

Firm: That's a good assumption.

Interviewee: Now, if I remember correctly, you said that the products in the line ranged from $40 to $500/product—can I assume that that's similar to the rest of the specialty cookware market?

Firm: Sure.

Interviewee: The middle of that range is $270, and I'm going to assume that a household purchasing each year buys only one product, just to be a bit conservative in my market sizing. So, that's $270 spent each year by four million households. If you multiply those out, you get a total specialty cookware market size of $1.08 billion.

Firm: That seems reasonable—maybe a bit high, but our client is hoping to grow the market as well as its share if it makes this investment. Now, getting back to the question of the case: Should the client buy the rights?

Interviewee: Well, if I remember correctly, you said that the client would only consider buying the rights if it could achieve a revenue of $50 million in the first five years. That's only a 5 percent market share in five years, which seems

© 2008 Vault.com Inc.

doable but aggressive. Does the PE client have any expertise in marketing new brands?

Firm: Actually, it does. The PE firm has a really great marketing company that it works with and believes that it could get 5 percent of the specialty kitchenware market in the U.S. within five years.

Interviewee: Well, if that's the case, then even if my market sizing is off, the client's goals do seem achievable and it should purchase the rights to the brand in the U.S.

Firm: That's great. We're done.

Telecom Equipment/Services Provider Case

A large telecom equipment provider has seen its profitability decline in recent years. It has hired us to find out why and help it turn around its profitability. How would you structure our response?

Additional information provided during questioning

• The client is a global telecom equipment/services provider. It is based in the U.S., but it serves a global customer group.

• The client serves primarily business customers, like large global corporations that need their own global networks, dedicated lines, etc. However, it has started to serve home offices for global business customers and developed small office/home office product lines and operations in markets where those are quite prevalent.

• The global telecom industry surged in the 1990s, but in recent years, due to a tremendous supply in global telecom capacity, demand for telecom equipment dropped quickly. All traditional global telecom manufacturers and suppliers were hit hard by this turn in the market.

• The client has traditionally gotten 80 percent of its revenue from itstelecom equipment manufacturing business and 20 percent from its installation/maintenance and services business.

Visit the Vault Consulting Career Channel at **www.vault.com/consulting** — with insider firm profiles, message boards, the Vault Consulting Job Board and more.

VAULT CAREER LIBRARY   **159**

Suggested high-level overview of solution

While this is a profitability case, and the interviewee should layout the structure in terms of the two levers of profitability, an industry analysis using Porter's Five Forces or the three Cs is really the only way to drive to the actual answer to the case. Both frameworks are laid out, though using the three Cs is probably the simplest. Hypothesis generation and testing is one of the other tools used in this case. Consultants frequently use this with clients; so, the interviewer brings it up here to see how adept the interviewee is at applying it in this situation.

This is not a quantitative case. There's also not a lot of information in this case. The interviewee really has to use his or her imagination to keep generating ideas—no matter how frustrating that gets—in order to get to an answer. Using several frameworks to structure the problem and generate ideas is really the way to get at the answer.

Breakdown of solution (including quantitative analyses and qualitative evaluations)

Interviewee: Let me just make sure that I understand the case setup correctly. Our client is a large telecom equipment manufacturer and provider that has seen its profitability decline in recent years, and it has hired us to help them figure out how to turn that around?

Firm: Yes. That's right. How would you approach that problem? Take a few minutes if you need them.

(Few minutes go by ...)

Interviewee: Well, this seems like a standard profitability case to me. The two levers of profitability are revenue and costs. Within revenue, you want to look at whether the price of our offering has changed, or whether the volume of how much we sell has changed. Within costs, you can look at whether the fixed costs of the company have changed, or whether the variable costs have changed. Or, we could run down the items of the income statement to see if there are any major changes there.

© 2008 Vault.com Inc.

(Below is the way to lay out this structure.)

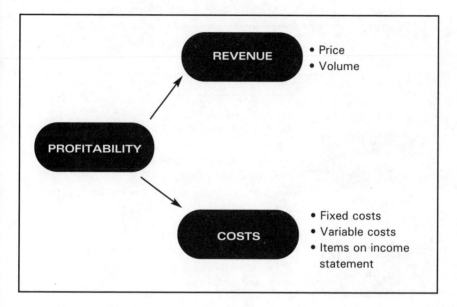

Firm: That's right. Now, I can tell you from the client's own knowledge that nothing has changed on the costs side. So, the changes have definitely happened on the revenue side. Where does that take your thinking?

Interviewee: Well, then either the volume has decreased or the price has decreased. I imagine that the client would know if price had decreased; so, I'll assume that volume has decreased.

Firm: That's right. So, how would you evaluate looking into why volume has declined for the client?

Interviewee: Can I have a few minutes to collect my thoughts?

Firm: Of course. Just let me know when you're ready.

(Few minutes go by ...)

Interviewee: Well, you would need to do some sort of industry analysis to understand why the client's volume is declining. I tend to approach these things by dividing my analysis into four main buckets: 1) company/product changes, 2) customer satisfaction, 3) competitive landscape, and 4) overall market dynamics/setting.

Visit the Vault Consulting Career Channel at **www.vault.com/consulting** — with insider firm profiles, message boards, the Vault Consulting Job Board and more.

VAULT CAREER LIBRARY   **161**

(Below is an illustration of this approach using the framework described, and an approach using Porter's Five Forces framework (on page 163). The Five Forces are not used throughout the rest of the case but are shown here as an example of another approach that an interviewee could take.)

COMPANY

Has our company changed its products or services in some way that has made us lose business?
- Different product offering? Different product composition?

Has our company failed to innovate in the market, or keep up with the competition?

CUSTOMERS

Have the customers decreased?
- Have customers gone elsewhere?
- Have we stopped serving a customer need

Have customers started spending less?

Are there new customers that we should go pursue?

COMPETITORS

Who is our competition?
- Are there numerous competitors? Or have market shares remained fairly stable?

Has competition increased recently? Are new competitors predictable or unexpected?

MARKET SETTING/ DYNAMICS

Is the market for telecom equipment growing or shrinking?
- What's been the recent trend? What's been the long-term trend?
- Have there been market-changing events/ inventions recently?

Is this a local or global market? Are there new markets left to enter/expand into that are as yet untapped?

© 2008 Vault.com Inc.

THREAT OF NEW ENTRANTS	• Are new entrants likely? Have there already been new entrants? • Are there any barriers to entry? • Patented technology? • Government regulation?
BUYER POWER	• Are the number of buyers concentrated, or diffused? • How many buyers are there in the market? • Is the number of buyers growing or shrinking? • Has negotiating power on the buyer side recently increased for some reason? • Has there been government intervention to increase buying power?
RIVALRY	• Has rivalry increased in the market? • Are market shares changing because of increased rivalry? • Has competition increased?
SUBSTITUTES/ COMPLEMENTS	• Are there substitutes to our product that now exist in the market? • Are there complements to our product category that could stabilize our share, or that are increasing rivalry?
SUPPLIER POWER	• Have suppliers increased in power? • Have the suppliers increased or decreased? • Are key suppliers working more in tandem with our competition than with us? • Are suppliers vertically integrating, increasing competition in the industry?

Firm: That's great. You've brought up a lot of questions for analysis. But instead of just asking questions, do you have any hypotheses about what might be going on here in those four buckets?

Interviewee: Sure. Can I take a few minutes just to write them out?

Firm: Of course.

(A few minutes go by ...)

Visit the Vault Consulting Career Channel at **www.vault.com/consulting** — with insider firm profiles, message boards, the Vault Consulting Job Board and more.

VAULT CAREER LIBRARY   **163**

Interviewee: Well, I have several. They are …

COMPANY	• Hypothesis: The company has changed its product offering and no longer meets customers' needs. • Hypothesis: The company has failed to innovate to keep up with the competition
CUSTOMERS	• Hypothesis: There are fewer customers because our typical customers have gone to the competition. • Hypothesis: Our customers have started to spend less on our category.
COMPETITORS	• Hypothesis: Competition has increased, driving prices down. • Hypothesis: Competition has increased, fragmenting the market. • Hypothesis: Unexpected competition has entered our market with new substitutes for our category/product line.
MARKET SETTING/ DYNAMICS	• Hypothesis: The telecom equipment market is shrinking. • Hypothesis: The telecom equipment market is growing, but not in the markets that we are in. • Hypothesis: The telecom equipment market has slowed, due to a recession or some other unforeseen market force.

Firm: That's a pretty comprehensive list. Now, before we dive into that list and get at the client's problem, can you tell me what data sources you might look at to prove or disprove each of those hypotheses? Take a couple of minutes, or brainstorm out loud—whatever you're more comfortable with.

Interviewee: Sure, let me collect my thoughts for a minute … OK, so I have the following list:

© 2008 Vault.com Inc.

COMPANY
- Company's product offering over time vs. competition's product offering over time
- Surveys of customer satisfaction
- Company's market share

CUSTOMERS
- Customer surveys
- Customer annual reports
- Lit searches and analyst reports for industry
- Trade journals for industry
- Number of customer companies (has this grown, or shrunk?)

COMPETITORS
- Number of telecom equipment manufacturers from an industry board or trade publication
- Market shares from industry reports
- Lit searches and analyst reports on industry/competition
- Annual reports of competition

MARKET SETING/ DYNAMICS
- Lit searches and analyst reports on industry/competition
- Interviews with industry thought leaders
- Interviews/surveys with customers
- Annual reports of competition

Firm: That's great. Now, back to your hypotheses. Where would you like to start in tackling this problem?

Interviewee: In terms of the company, maybe it has changed its key product or service, which has led to a decrease in volume, or maybe it hasn't changed its product offering to keep up with the competition or the innovation happening in the market.

Firm: That's a good couple of hypotheses. Unfortunately, we looked a bit at that, and the client's offering is the same as its competitors in the market. Let me tell you a bit more about the client. It's a global telecom equipment/services provider based in the U.S., but it serves a global customer group. The client serves primarily business customers, like large global corporations that need their own global networks, dedicated lines, etc. However, it has started to serve home offices for global business customers, and developed small office/home office product lines and operations in markets where those are quite prevalent. Does that give you any further insight?

Interviewee: Actually, yes. I take from that that competition isn't really the problem here. I mean, one of my hypotheses had been that new competition had entered the market, taking customers away from us, or introducing substitutes in the market that has decreased demand. But now I'm thinking that the competition has little to do with the client's problems.

Firm: You're right. We looked there, too. And it seemed that the competition was facing similar problems to those of our client. What other hypotheses do you want to explore?

Interviewee: Well, you mentioned that our client serves a global customer group, and that we've primarily served business customers, but are starting to serve consumers with home offices. Have we somehow driven our normal customer base away by starting to serve consumers? Or, if I go back to my hypotheses, are our business customers just spending less on telecom equipment than they used to?

Firm: Now you're really getting somewhere. Customers are spending less on the telecom equipment category. You see, what we found was that the global telecom industry surged in the 1990s, but in recent years, due to a tremendous supply in global telecom capacity, demand for telecom equipment dropped quickly. All traditional global telecom manufacturers and suppliers were hit hard by this turn in the market.

Interviewee: So, it's my last bucket then—there are marketwide dynamics that have caused the client's decline in volume, declines in sales, and decline in profitability.

Firm: Yes. But what do you suggest for it to do to fix the problem? How do you suggest that it grows its revenue?

Interviewee: Well, the first thing that comes to mind is targeting a new type of consumer. You mentioned that the client typically sold its equipment to business customers, but that it is starting to sell its products to consumers with home offices. Can it grow that business in any way?

Firm: That's a good hunch. And yes, it can. But we didn't want to just tell the client that for two reasons: 1) it's already growing its consumer segment; so, it doesn't add much value for us to just tell the client to continue doing something that it is already doing, and 2) because of its product line and the size of the two markets, there's no way that it could make up for all of its lost revenue from the business customer market in the consumer market. Any other ways that it might be able to restore its revenue?

© 2008 Vault.com Inc.

Interviewee: Well, if it can't just restore revenue by targeting a different customer type, is there a new geographic market that it could enter for its business customers?

Firm: That's a good thought, too. But unfortunately, it's already a global player—most markets have already been tapped.

Interviewee: Can it start to do something that it hasn't done before, like manufacture a different type of product?

Firm: That's another good thought, too. But it needs solutions for its profitability now, and changing what it manufactures and brings to market will take years for it to see substantial revenue from that investment.

Interviewee: Well, if it can't enter a new product market and can't enter a new customer market, is there something else that it's now doing that it could grow, which I haven't considered?

Firm: You're on the right track. What capabilities, other than manufacturing telecom products, does the client have?

Interviewee: If I review my notes, I believe you said that it's a global telecom equipment manufacturer and services provider. Wait, that's it. What kind of services does it provide?

Firm: Good question. The client has traditionally gotten 80 percent of its revenue from its telecom equipment manufacturing business and 20 percent from its installation/maintenance and services business. What does that make you think?

Interviewee: Is there any way that it can grow its services business? I mean, business customers may have enough capacity and equipment, but maybe the client could use more servicing and maintenance of that equipment?

Firm: You're right. That's it. And that's what we recommended to the client.

Wondering what it's like to work at a specific employer?

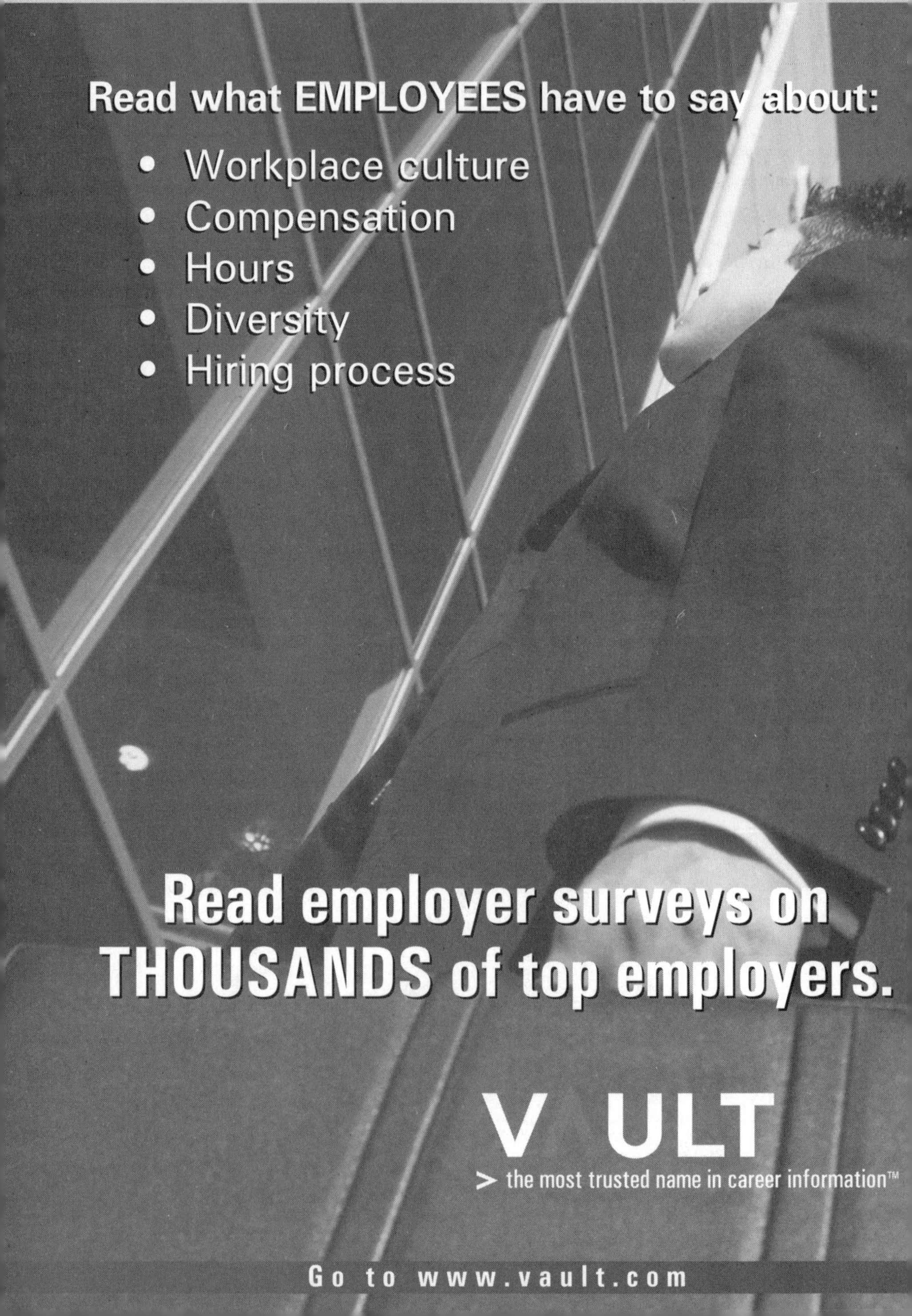

CAREER
GUIDE

FINAL
ANALYSIS

CASE INTERVIEW
PRACTICE
GUIDE

© 2008 Vault.com Inc.

Final Analysis

In conclusion, there are a few things to keep in mind not only as you prepare for your case interviews, but as you walk through the door to the interview.

First, practice will help you. Like any test, assignment or hurdle, practicing will make you more comfortable with the skill set, better at the problems and more able to surpass the hurdle. Practice may never make you perfect—most consultants will tell you that they'd probably do horribly if given a case interview today, but they were likely much better at them when they were preparing for all of their case interviews.

Second, practicing cases and going to case interviews will in many ways help you understand if you want to be a consultant. If you find case interviewing wholly miserable, then maybe consulting isn't right for you—either way, working through this book is an important step to helping you figure that out.

Third, while you can practice for years and become the master of every style of case interviewing, there's one thing to keep in mind: the one thing that you kind of can't prepare for, but should prepare for, is the unexpected. Case interviewers get tired and cut the case short. Case interviewers get bored, stop giving the prescribed case and start giving a brainteaser instead. A seasoned case interviewer gets called away to a client meeting at the last minute, and a consultant who has never given a case interview before in his life gets called to stand in and be your interviewer. You may not have the most perfect interview setting when you interview—but you don't have much control of that! What you do have control over is how you react to it: if you're flexible, calm, good-natured and helpful through it all, well, then you may just show how you're the perfect consultant: still being smart and personable even when your flight home from the client site is canceled.

Finally, it never hurts to just keep your fingers crossed, have a little luck and keep things in perspective. If you practice and work through the cases in this book, you will have done more than many other applicants and probably be better prepared than most—and with a little luck, you'll do great and get the job!

GO FOR THE GOLD!

GET VAULT GOLD MEMBERSHIP AND GET ACCESS TO ALL OF VAULT'S AWARD-WINNING CONSULTING CAREER INFORMATION

◆ **Employee surveys** for top consulting firms, with insider info on
  - Company culture
  - Salaries and compensation
  - Hiring process and interviews
  - Business outlook

◆ Access to **100 + extended insider consulting firm profiles**

◆ **Vault's exclusive consulting firm rankings,** including quality of life and practice area rankings

◆ Insider consulting salary information with **Vault's Consulting Salary Central**

◆ **Student and alumni surveys** for 100s of top MBA programs and law schools

◆ Access to **complete Vault message board archives**

◆ **15% off** all Vault purchases, including Vault Guides, Consulting Employer Profiles and Case Interview Prep

For more information go to
www.vault.com/consulting

VAULT
> the most trusted name in career info

APPENDIX

V/\ULT CAREER LIBRARY

© 2008 Vault.com Inc.

Sample Guesstimates/ Brainteasers

- How many telephone booths are there in Manhattan?

- How many manhole covers are there in Manhattan?

- How many cell phones are there in the U.S.? How many residential landlines are there in the U.S.? How many business landlines are there in the U.S.?

- How many cups of coffee are consumed in the U.S. on a daily basis? How many are sold at Starbucks vs. Dunkin' Donuts? How many are consumed at home vs. outside the home?

- How many elementary school textbooks are used in the U.S. on a daily basis?

- How many K-12 school teachers are there in the U.S.?

- How many credit cards are there in the U.S.?

- How many televisions are there in the U.S.?

- How many iPods are there in the U.S.?

- How many cars are there in the U.S.?

- How many new cars are purchased each year in the U.S.?

- How many pets are there in the U.S.? How many dogs? How many cats?

- How many cans of cat food are sold in the U.S. on a weekly basis?

- How many cans of soup are sold on the U.S. per month on average?

- How much do you think Home Depot's sales will grow next year?

- How much do you think Wal-Mart's sales will grow next year?

- How much do you think Starbucks's sales will grow next year?

- How much do you think Pfizer's sales will grow next year?

- How much to you think Universal Music's sales will grow next year?

- What will the price of a cup of Starbucks coffee be in five years?

- What will the price of a gallon of milk be in 10 years?

Data points to know for brainteasers:

- Population of the U.S.: 300 million (this could range from 250 to 300 million, so make your assumption clear)

- Number of households in the U.S.: 100 million (this could range from 100 to 150 million, so make your assumption clear)

- Annual GDP growth in U.S.: 3 to 5 percent

© 2008 Vault.com Inc.

Sample Non-Case Interview Questions

Walk me through your resume and explain how it's led you to be here today

Follow-ups/other versions:

- Tell me more about your role at Company X. How did that grow/change over time? Why did you leave?

- Your last two jobs are in completely different fields/functions—why is that? What connects them?

- You seem to have moved around a lot. Why have you not stayed at any one job for very long?

- Why did you decide to take a job at Company X?

- X job seems like a step down. Why did you decide to take that job?

- You have a one-year gap on your resume. How do you explain that?

- Your results in job X are very impressive. How do you explain those? How much of that was a team effort vs. an individual effort?

- Tell me about how you chose the college that you attended. What was your process? What was your criteria in selecting that school?

- Tell me about any one of your past jobs that you think shows how you'd be good at this job.

- Where do you see yourself in five to 10 years?

- Is there anything on your resume that we haven't talked about that you'd like to talk about?

- What are you most proud of?

- Tell me something about yourself that's not on your resume.

Visit the Vault Consulting Career Channel at **www.vault.com/consulting**. — with insider firm profiles, message boards, the Vault Consulting Job Board and more.

VAULT CAREER LIBRARY   **177**

What are your strengths? What are your weaknesses?

Follow-ups/other versions:

• Tell me about a time that you failed.

• What would your last boss/team say were your strengths and weaknesses?

• What would your friends say were your strengths and weaknesses?

• What is the biggest challenge you've had to overcome? How did you rise to the occasion?

Tell me about a time where you had to change the opinion of a group

Follow-ups/other versions:

• What was your plan going in? How did that plan change over time? Why did it change?

• Was your opinion swayed by anyone else's over the course of the process?

• What would you do differently today? What did you learn from the process?

• Describe a situation where you had to be persuasive.

Describe a time when you did something differently than it had been done before

Follow-ups/other versions:

• How did you convince others that this new way of doing things was good/better?

• What did your new process achieve that couldn't have been had you done it the old way?

• What have you done that's innovative?

• Would you describe yourself as an entrepreneur?

• Have you ever founded a new organization or team?

• Tell me about a time that you approached an analytical problem creatively?

• Describe your creative skills.

© 2008 Vault.com Inc.

Tell me about a time when you worked as part of a team

Follow-ups/other versions:

• Tell me about a time that you had to work in a cross-functional team.

• Tell me about a time when you didn't agree with the direction/leadership of the team. How did you handle it? What would you have done differently? What did you learn during the process?

• Tell me about a time that you had to manage conflict at work. How did you handle it? What would you have done differently? What did you learn during the process?

• Tell me about a time that you had to manage a team/group of people.

• How do you foster teamwork?

• Describe a setting in which you used your leadership skills.

How do you manage risk?

Follow-ups/other versions:

• Give me an example of a shortcut that you took to get something done.

• Describe a time when you took a calculated risk. How did it turn out? Would you do it again?

• Tell me about a time that you had to manage risk and how you dealt with it.

• Describe a situation where you faced an ethical dilemma. How did you handle it? Is there anything you would have done differently?

Why should I hire you?

Follow-ups/other versions:

• What one thing makes you different from all the other candidates here today? All the other people at your school?

• What would you specifically bring to my company/team?

• If I were a student at your school, why would I want you on my team?

• Are you a leader, a team player or a creative type? What are some examples that demonstrate that?

Visit the Vault Consulting Career Channel at **www.vault.com/consulting.** — with insider firm profiles, message boards, the Vault Consulting Job Board and more.

VAULT CAREER LIBRARY   **179**

• How would you describe yourself?

Why this company/firm?

Follow-ups/other versions:

• Why not one of our competitors? How are we different? Why are you most suited to/interested in us?

• What criteria are you using to evaluate the firms that you're looking at?

• How do you think you will fit into the culture here? How would you describe the culture here?

• Who have you talked to/met with so far at the firm?

• When/how did you first hear about us?

• If you don't end up working here, where will you go?

• What other firms are you looking at?

• What do you see as the most important issues this organization will address in the next five years?

• Why consulting/strategic planning/corporate or business development?

Acing the Case:
Checklist

Having the Correct Mindset is Key to Acing the Case Interview

Think like you are actually the consultant on the case

- Come equipped with the 10 different frameworks you have practiced and memorized. Really listen to the problem as if you are the consultant or client involved, and think about how you will actually solve the problem. Try to bucket ideas in a MECE (mutually exclusive comprehensively exhaustive) way, and in a natural fashion (i.e., logic tree). Trying to force a framework onto a case is a clear path to being dinged.

- Engage the interview and drive the case forward. Get into the driver's seat and ask the right questions, ask for data, and share insights. The person giving you the case is also analyzing what it would be like to work with you in a team situation—give him or her the chance to guide you, too.

Think like a CEO or a Partner

- Try to take a step back when developing and forming a framework to proceed with the case. Should you actually cover everything that is important? Are you too detail-oriented? Are you thinking like a partner, CEO or owner of the business? Always take a step back mentally and make sure you are actually answering the case question itself.

Customize your approach to the interviewers

- For the first rounds, you may have to be more detail-focused and prove you can do the math. The standard timing is: developing framework/logic tree with clarifying questions, one to two minutes. Driving to solution: 20 to 25 minutes. Conclusion: one minute.

- For the second/final rounds, be sensitive to the interviewers. A senior partner may be more interested in whether you can think like a partner or CEO rather than how you crunch the numbers or cross the Ts and dot the Is. Focus on having an intelligent, structured discussion and engaging the partners/senior partners.

- The case interviews are really good indicators of the problem-solving aspects of consulting. Think about if you actually like the ambiguity, researching different industries and business areas all the time. If you really do not like the case interview process, and even if you do them really well, consulting may not be for you.

Assess whether you are having fun

Proper Framework Development is Critical for Success

Answer the question

- Do you know the key questions? Make sure you answer the question before coming up with the framework. Don't sidestep answering the question because you think another area is more interesting.

Prioritize your framework

- To push the case ahead, explain those areas you are planning to focus on first and why you chose these areas. Being 80/20 is extremely important in the case interview, given the limited time you have. You may not be right, but at least the consultant knows you are pushing the case forward.

Refer back to your framework

- Your framework is your path to solving the case. Try to refer to it when you finish analyzing a discrete piece of information.

- If you realize your framework is wrong in the first 10 minutes of the interview, try to revise your framework or create a new one so that you can still ace the interview.

© 2008 Vault.com Inc.

Organize, Calculate and Communicate

- WRITE BIG so the interviewer can read your notes from across the desk! If he can read what you write, the consultant can then follow your train of thought and give you helpful hints along the way.

Proper Paper Management

- Organize your papers properly (page #1: case information and logic tree, page #2: details/calculations from branch 1, page #3: from another branch, last page: conclusion or page #1 logic tree with supporting facts).

- Use more sheets of paper rather than less, and use a new sheet of paper for each discrete module of analysis. Now is not the time to save trees.

- Practice your mental math. Read *How to Calculate* quickly by Henry Sticker. Strong mental math will help you to conduct quick sanity check on your calculations, and remain calm when met with an avalanche of calculations. You should be able to calculate 95% of $450 in two seconds. If not, read the book!

Math! Math! Math!

- Be organized in calculating your data. Explain what calculation you plan to do **before** doing them. Write down all the variables involved in thecalculation so the consultant can follow what you are doing. Designate the bottom part of the paper to do the detailed calculations (but you can avoid these if you are good with mental math).

- Practice the Pyramid Principle (by Barbara Minto). Give the answer first and then your reasoning. Giving the answer sets the context for the reasoning, and also helps the interviewer to focus on what you are saying.

Be structured in thinking and talking

- Try to communicate in point forms so your logic is easy to follow. For example, there are three areas I want to look into, there are two reasons for this change, I think there are three issues in this problem, etc. Don't babble a stream of consciousness. Remember the interviewer may have interviewed six students before you!

Getting Unstuck and Ending Perfectly

When stuck, imagine you are actually in the situation

- If you get stuck, take a step back and visualize yourself in the specific situation. Imagine yourself as the consumer looking at the products on the shelves, imagine yourself as the CEO of the company, imagine yourself as the worker operating that machinery on the floor. Putting yourself in the specific situation can help you to think of possible options you might never have thought about.

Summarize the situation the way a CEO wants to hear it

- Spend a few minutes recollecting the interview in preparation for your recommendation

- Give the answers first, then your rationales. Prioritize which of the solutions you recommend implementing first (80/20).

- Use relevant data and insights from the last 20 to 30 minutes to support your rationale.

- Talk about any major considerations for the relevant solutions, and talk about other potential areas to look at.

- Keep recommendations in point form, and keep all of these under one minute (max).

© 2008 Vault.com Inc.

Visit the Vault Consulting Career Channel at **www.vault.com/consulting.** — with insider firm profiles, message boards, the Vault Consulting Job Board and more.

VAULT CAREER LIBRARY   185

About the Authors

Rishi Marwah is a Management Consultant in the Singapore office of a global management consultancy firm. An MBA graduate of the Joseph L. Rotman School of Management (Toronto), he has advised clients in Europe and Southeast Asia. Earlier in his career, he was involved in two startups in Toronto.

Sridhar Parameshwaran is an Associate with A. T. Kearney working out of the London office. He graduated from Kellogg in 2006 with majors in Strategy and Marketing. Prior to Kellogg, Sridhar spent four years working with i2 Technologies as a product manager dealing with supply chain issues.

Robert Vujovich is a Principal with Celenium Group, LLC. He has more than 25 years of diverse industry, information technology, and management consulting experience, particularly in the areas of IT outsourcing, service line portfolio management, manufacturing and product engineering. While a principal management consultant with A.T. Kearney, Bob focused on developing client relationships, account planning and engagement execution. Bob also served as ATK's University of Michigan graduate business school campus recruiting officer.

© 2008 Vault.com Inc.

Losing sleep over your job search?
Endlessly revising your resume?
Facing a work-related dilemma?

Named the
"Top Choice" by
The Wall Street Journal
for resume
makeovers

"We got the best revamp from Vault.com. Our expert pronounc the resume 'perfect.'"

The Wall Street Journ

"I have rewritten this resume 12 times and in one review you to the essence of what I wanted to say!" – *S.G. Atlanta, GA*

Vault Resume Writing

On average, a hiring manager weeds through 120 resumes for a single job opening. Let our experts write your resume from scratch to make sure it stands out.

- Start with an e-mailed history and 1- to 2-hour phone discussion
- Vault experts will create a first draft
- After feedback and discussion, Vault experts will deliver a final draft, ready for submission

Vault Resume Review

- Submit your resume online
- Receive an in-depth e-mailed critique with suggestions on revisions within TWO BUSINESS DAYS

Vault Career Coach

Whether you are facing a major career change or dealing with a workplace dilemma, our experts can help you make the most educated decision via telephone counseling sessions.

- Sessions are 45-minutes over the telephone

"It was well worth the price! I have bee struggling with this for weeks and in 48 hours you had given me the answers! I know what I need to change." – *T.H. Pasadena, CA*

> the most trusted name in career information™

For more information go
www.vault.com/careerc

Get the BUZZ on Top Schools

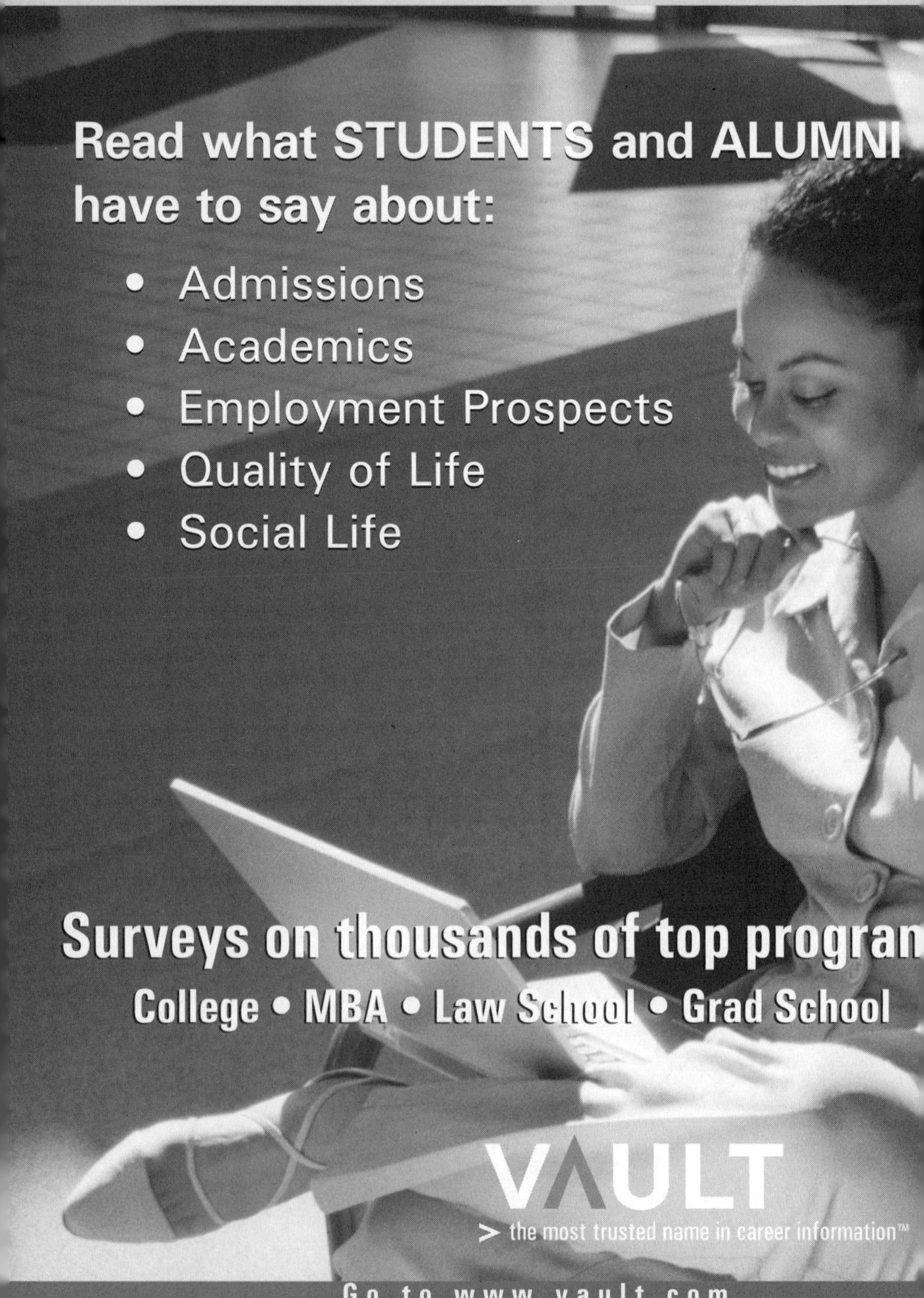

Go to www.vault.com